Law for the
Medical Practitioner

Law for the Medical Practitioner

Charles W. Quimby, Jr., M.D., LL.B.

AUPHA PRESS
Ann Arbor, Michigan • Washington, D.C.

Copyright © 1979 by the Regents of The University of Michigan

Library of Congress Cataloging in Publication Data

Quimby, Charles W
    Law for the medical practitioner.

    Includes index.
    1. Medical laws and legislation — United States.
    2. Physicians — Malpractice — United States.
    I. Title.
    KF3821.Q55   344'.73'041   79-22965
    ISBN 0-914904-39-6

80 81 82 83/6 5 4 3 2

AUPHA Press   Washington D.C. and Ann Arbor, Michigan

This book is dedicated to
Dean John E. Chapman, M.D.
and
Professor Bradley E. Smith, M.D.
for their help, support, and encouragement.

Preface

The physician can expect to be drawn into increasingly more contact with the lawyer and bureaucrat. The physician's basic and professional training does not equip him to understand the lawyer's methods or the salient points of law that may impale the physician. This primer's aim is to equip the physician with the tools to dispassionately analyze a patient-physician or hospital-physician fact situation from several points of view.

This primer is not designed to make a lawyer out of a doctor. It is designed to alert the physician to seek competent legal advice as soon as he spots a *potential* legal conflict.

A book can set forth the salient points of law and the ways in which they can be applied, and the legal method can be outlined. But the physician can only savor the aggressive nature of the adversary legal system when he receives a summons and complaint, is examined and cross-examined at deposition and on the witness stand. The abrasive aspects of the adversary system may not only disconcert and repulse the physician but also arouse his righteous anger and indignation. These reactions are not conducive to resolving a dispute legally and equitably; on the contrary, they are counterproductive. This primer is designed to help the physician avoid these very reactions.

Case reports are used in an attempt to show how the lawyer functions. They are used sparingly in the early chapters in order not to overwhelm the reader. In the later chapters, their use is increased to show the tenor of the judges' thinking in developing areas of the law, and to give the reader some idea of the direction in which law is steering medicine, and also of what society expects of the physician.

Because there is no word in English that refers to the human being (singular) without regard to gender, I have generally used the traditional masculine singular pronoun when referring to a person whose gender is unknown and totally irrelevant to the context.

. . .

I wish to gratefully acknowledge all the benefits I have derived from the incisive and abrasive arguments with Professor Frederic K. Spies of the University of Arkansas Law School at Little Rock about medical malpractice and medical causation versus legal causation. I also wish to thank Professor D. Fenton Adams of the University of Arkansas Law School at Little Rock for his criticism of the chapter on Contracts — any errors are mine, not his, and Professor A. Everett James of Vanderbilt University School of Medicine for reading the manuscript. Finally, I am indebted to my wife, Lois H. Quimby, for her support and help in the criticism, editing, and typing of the many versions of this manuscript.

Charles W. Quimby, Jr.
Nashville, Tennessee
July, 1979

Contents

Chapter One

Introduction to the Adversary System

I

Whether at the tribal or clan level or in a complex modern society, any legal system is designed to settle disputes once and for all and, at the same time, keep peace in the community. How disputes are settled depends in part upon the size, needs, history, and sophistication of the community. Under the American legal system, civil disputes that the parties are unable to settle among themselves can be settled with finality by resort to a lawsuit and trial.

A trial under this legal system is an adversary procedure. If the trial is viewed through the misty veil of history, one can see two champions tilting and jousting on the plain under the watchful eyes of the referee, the townspeople, and the local feudal official (perhaps the king). The rationale for the adversary form of the trial is that it is the best way to find the truth. What we see at trial today is an extremely highly refined adversary procedure before a judge who acts as referee for the adversaries and gives the law to the jury, which finds the facts (truths), applies the law to the facts, and renders a verdict for one side and against the other. The verdict settles the dispute.

Due Process

The jury verdict, however, is not quite the end of the story. The losing party has the right of appeal to a higher court, called an appellate (appeals) court. Depending upon the jurisdiction (state or federal), there may be one or two appellate courts. By tradition or by constitutional creation, or both, these courts review the record of the trial court for errors of law, not fact. If no error is found, the appellate court affirms the judgment of the trial court; the dispute is at an end, settled. If the appellate courts find errors of law, or bias, passion, or prejudice on the part of the judge or jury, they can reverse the judgment of the trial court and send the case back for a new trial.

To enter the legal system, the lawyer for one of the parties (in civil cases, the person who starts the lawsuit is called the plaintiff; his opponent the defendant) files papers (a complaint), which set forth the plaintiff's side of the controversy with the clerk of the *court* that has the *power to settle such disputes*. At the same time, a formal written *notice* of the suit, accompanied by a copy of the complaint, is served on the defendant, which lets him know of the suit. The defendant then has a certain time to reply. When he replies to the complaint, the issue is joined. Then the parties have an opportunity to collect more information through written interrogatories, oral depositions, and other discovery procedures. Generally, after all this, there is a pre-trial conference that seeks either to settle the case without a trial or, failing that, to clearly define, reduce, and narrow the issues at dispute to be settled at trial.

At trial, both sides present testimony of their witnesses as well as tangible evidence and have an opportunity to cross-examine the opposing witnesses.

In addition to the mechanics of the legal system, the foregoing describes the bulwark of America's freedom: procedural due process. This means the defendant shall have *notice* of the trial before an *impartial tribunal* that has the *power to settle the issues at trial*. He shall have the opportunity to *hear* the evidence against him, *confront* (cross-examine) his accusers, and *present evidence in his own defense*. Concisely, it's fairness.

Precedent

The American legal system is a common law system except for Louisiana. This means that each case is decided on its own merits but guided by rulings in similar prior cases. Early in the development of our legal system, the members of a community saw or knew the legal outcome of the defendant's behavior; they were likely, depending on the facts of the case, either to avoid doing what the defendant did or to do what the defendant should have done. Each person knew if he did what the defendant did, he'd receive the same punishment. In other words, the prior case would control the court's analysis of a later defendant's similar behavior. Restated: the prior case would be a precedent for the second and following cases.

In legal terminology, each case is said to have a holding. For example, farmer agrees to sell a horse to doctor for $500. Doctor sues farmer to get the horse before paying the $500. The court says: farmer doesn't have to give the horse to doctor until he pays farmer the $500. As a precedent, this case would control the same or similar cases coming later. In legal parlance, the case holds that, in a cash transaction, the buyer must pay the money to the seller and the seller must accept the money before the seller is obligated to turn over the subject matter of the transaction to the buyer.

Semantics

Note carefully the language used to describe two very live people arguing heatedly over two perfectly real and tangible things: $500 and a horse. The holding of the case is written in dry, abstract, all inclusive language. The case has been drained of its emotion, but the formal procedures at trial are designed to do just that. By altering the slant and choice of words, the case could have restricted the articulation of the legal precedent (the case's holding) to horses, $500 sales, sales between farmers and doctors, farmer-sellers only, doctor-buyers only. The latter is ridiculous, but the others aren't.

The discussion began with legal precedents and ended with a look at the lawyer's forte: the use of words (semantics). Semantics is not generally the physician's forte. However, in managing legal problems, the physician reader must become adept at listening to and reading words critically. As an advocate, the lawyer in serving his client tries to lead his listeners, judge, jury, and others, to a given position beneficial to his side. It is the opposing lawyer's job to expose the other lawyer's argument for what it is, by offering other evidence or by showing that the bias and slant of the other attorney's words does not clearly and factually describe the situation. Most of this is done with the use of words.

An important point to remember here is that, although one attorney chooses to slant his argument away from the other side by his choice of words, this is not dishonest. There is a huge gap between advocacy and dishonesty. After all, the lawyer is paid to advocate the best point of view of a situation for his client. And of course the opposing attorney has the same opportunity to present the case in its best light by his choice of words.

Here, we come to the problem of the opposing attorneys' relative abilities. However, inept advocates don't last too long; silver tongued advocates do lose cases, juries can cut through the words pretty well, and the appeals process largely avoids the problem. Appellate judges are experts at words or they wouldn't be there. In short, the law tries to keep this factor to a minimum.

Bad Law

Times change. A precedent perfectly appropriate for one era may be useless in another. If the situation that called for the rule of law or precedent doesn't arise anymore, the rule of law is lost and forgotten. If the situation does arise and the precedent is applied, even though changed circumstances make its application unjust, the result is said to be bad law, a euphemism for one or both parties to the lawsuit being unjustly treated.

Blind adherence to precedent has occurred and will occur. One solution is for the legislature to enact a statute covering the situation that is consonant with current legal, social, economic, or political mores. The highest state court can repudiate unjust precedents by fashioning a new rule of law, modifying the precedent to fit current mores, or by modifying its application. All four ways or combinations of them have been used to keep the common law in line with changing mores.

Since these rules of law guide people's behavior and people look to the rules of law for this guidance, judges and lawyers are not too anxious to change the rules of law too fast. On the other hand, were such rules to change rapidly, they'd be useless. Therefore, it might be said that a certain amount of conservatism is built into any viable legal system.

Rules of Law

By collecting many cash transaction cases, each of which will be a little different, and analyzing them, a trend or pattern can be seen in the decisions. From these trends, a general rule or principle of law can be articulated that will cover most cash transactions. By collecting the rules of law for different kinds of sales and for different kinds of subject matter, a body of law can be developed relating to the sale of goods. Put these rules together and publish them, and the title could be The Law of Sales. This is just what has been done over the years.

The words used to set forth the rules or principles of law are not as set and as precise as those in a statute. In a statute, the legislature writes out and adopts a certain set of words, which are exact and reproducible; they don't change unless the legislature changes them. On the other hand, each successive generation of lawyers can express the rules or principles of common law in the language of the times.

Procedural Law

Procedural law is a body of law regulating the initiation of a lawsuit, the conduct of a trial, admission of evidence, and the mechanism for appeals. Those rules of law governing institution of a lawsuit and the conduct of a trial are called civil procedure (the procedure for criminal cases has a somewhat different set of rules). Those rules governing the admission or exclusion of evidence are called the rules of evidence, many of which deal with exceptions to the hearsay rule.

The following is an example of hearsay evidence. One side puts on the stand a witness to prove the car involved in the accident was a peppermint-striped VW. Witness says, under oath, "Mr. X said a peppermint-striped VW caused the accident." That's no good; it's hearsay. Mr. X is not under oath as a witness and not subject to cross-examination. Witness's testimony can be kept out of evidence as hearsay.

A patient's clinical record is hearsay unless the writer of that portion of it under discussion is or has been a witness under oath and subject to cross-examination.

Most people are unfamiliar with rules of procedural law because they are highly technical. The application of these rules goes unnoticed at a trial unless looked for.

One procedural rule is that the plaintiff must present a *prima facie* case before the defendant is forced to present his defense. This means that the judge must be convinced that if the plaintiff's evidence is believed before the defendant has to put forth his case, the plaintiff would win the lawsuit. A prima facie case doesn't mean the plaintiff will win; the defendant's evidence may demolish the plaintiff's case. All it means is there is the possibility of his winning the lawsuit.

To find out what constitutes a prima facie case, reference is made to the facts and allegations in the complaint. If breach of contract is alleged, then the law of contracts is consulted; if slander, then the law of slander; if negligence, the law of negligence.

If the plaintiff does not present a prima facie case, his case is thrown out of court. He is said to be non-suited.

Res Ipsa Loquitur

One old procedural rule or doctrine has been rejuvenated for modern use. It is the doctrine of *res ipsa loquitur*, Latin for "the thing speaks for itself."

Here's the way it came about. Until quite recently, the plaintiff had to prove his entire case without resort to discovery devices (depositions, interrogatories, and discovery of documents) such as we have today. These devices permit the plaintiff to examine the defendant's witnesses, documents, and property before trial. One day in the early 1860s in England, plaintiff was walking on the sidewalk in front of a grain merchant's warehouse. From the second floor came a barrel of flour that injured the plaintiff. Plaintiff sued grain merchant. This outline is all plaintiff could show.

The defendant said, "I want a nonsuit because the plaintiff has not presented a prima facie case of negligence against me." Ordinarily, the defendant would have won. Even in those days that was pretty raw justice. Furthermore, barrels of flour don't generally come flying out of grain merchants' second floor windows. And everybody knows that if they do, somebody has been negligent in his duties.

The judge pointed out in the legal jargon of his time, which included some Latin, that some events are so likely to be caused by negligence, or to occur as a result of negligence, that the plaintiff does not have to present all the facts making out a prima facie case against the defendant. One can infer negligence of the particular event: res ipsa loquitur. This inference from the facts is sufficient to permit the judge (and later the jury, if necessary) to force the defendant to go forward with his defense.

This chapter has presented a brief, general overview of our legal system. Chapter Two introduces the concept of malpractice, which is of great interest and concern to the practicing physician.

Additional Reading

Edelman, M. *Political Language: Words that Succeed and Policies that Fail.* New York: Academic Press, 1977.

Hayakawa, S. I. *Language in Thought and Action.* 2d ed. New York: Harcourt, Brace, and Wild, 1964.

Pound, R. *The Spirit of the Common Law.* Boston: Marshall Jones Co., 1931.

Chapter
Two

Medical Malpractice

II

Today medical malpractice is not only a fact of the physician's professional life but an occupational hazard in some sections of the United States. Therefore, it is in the physician's best interests to understand what malpractice is and how to analyze a given set of facts for its potential.

Malpractice is negligence in the performance of a professional act.

Negligence

Broadly, negligence is a civil wrong (an unintentionally caused injury) in contradistinction to a criminal act (an intentionally caused injury). Society *punishes* the defendant for his criminal behavior by fine, loss of privilege (suspension of driver's license), loss of freedom (imprisonment), or loss of life (capital punishment). Society *compensates* the plaintiff injured by the negligent behavior of the defendant by forcing him to pay money damages to the plaintiff. Note the mild flavor of retribution but the full flavor of restitution in the preceding formulation of the rationale for money damages.

More narrowly, negligence is a highly technical term, a conclusion of law decided by a lawsuit. Negligence can be properly applied to a defendant's behavior only after the lawsuit alleging it has been decided against the defendant. Procedurally, the plaintiff must both allege *and prove*, if he can, to the court's satisfaction (judge and jury) that the defendant's behavior was negligent. Contrary to popular belief, the plaintiff's allegations don't establish the defendant's negligence. Therefore, institution of a negligence suit must not and ought not stigmatize the defendant.

Injury is both the prerequisite for a finding of and the rationale for negligence. No injury, no negligence. The rationale for the law of negligence is that every man is responsible for and should repair the damage he causes.

Drawing on society's experience with negligent behavior over the centuries, legal scholars have been able to articulate a concise formula for analyzing whether or not the defendant's behavior was negligent. This formula has two powerful uses. The first is anticipatory: to analyze a given fact situation for the potential of negligence, in other words, to *predict* that a court will more than likely hold the defendant liable for the plantiff's injury. The second is coldly practical: as a checklist of those indispensable elements the plaintiff must prove in court to hold the defendant guilty of negligence.

At the outset, it is mandatory for the reader to understand that, although the formula is useful, it can *only* be used *after* the events have occurred. It is precisely the lawyer's contemplative, retrospective analysis that irritates the physician. Because the physician is emotionally involved in the care of his patient and because he must make many crucial decisions under pressure, without the opportunity for quiet reflection, he feels that the lawyer and his client, the physician's former patient, are unfair to him. How else can it be done but retrospectively?

The physician's irritation with the lawyer and his client acts as a blind spot, which clouds the physician's analysis of a given fact situation for his or someone else's potential negligence. To prevent this blind spot from interfering with his analysis, the physician can either get a lawyer to analyze the situation for him, or step out of the shoes of the physician, or not identify with the physician-defendant. Once the physician overcomes this blind spot, he acquires a unique and detached vantage point from which to appraise his own patient-physician relationships in a more mature light and also to appreciate how society views the practice of medicine.

Analysis

The formula for analyzing whether or not the defendant's behavior was negligent is as follows: Defendant owed a

> DUTY to the plaintiff; the defendant's
> BREACH of that duty was the
> PROXIMATE CAUSE of the plaintiff's
> INJURY.

DUTY, as used here, is a highly abstract term. However, when analyzing a given fact situation, duty must be clearly and precisely spelled out for that fact situation. A precise articulation of the duty is not only a procedural necessity but also a safeguard against prejudice, emotion, and blind spots.

Duty covers three overlapping legal formulations of criteria for judging the defendant's behavior that is alleged to have caused the injury. One. The situation in which defendant finds himself vis-a-vis the plaintiff has taken place so many times that society has developed a successful way to deal with it. The implication is the defendant should know what is expected of him. This legal criterion's shorthand label is "standard of care."

Let us take several concrete examples to see where these standards come from.

Facts: It's noontime and the elementary school yard is full of children. The speed limit sign says, "15 MPH WHEN CHILDREN ARE PRESENT."

A. Defendant zips through at 55 mph. Child darts out into the street but defendant misses him. No injury; no negligence possible.

The sign clearly spells out the defendant's "duty." Also clear is the duty's rationale. Although the defendant didn't injure the child, he might get a ticket for speeding.

B. Same facts. Child darts out and speeding defendant injures him.

The defendant's duty is clearly spelled out by the traffic sign: when children are present, don't drive over 15 mph. The defendant drove more than 15 mph when children were present. By so doing he breached his duty to the plaintiff. His speeding was the direct, proximate, and immediate cause of the child's injury. In a negligence trial the defendant-driver would most probably be held negligent in injuring the child and, therefore, liable to the child (more correctly, to the child's parents) for the damages resulting from the injury.

C. Same facts. Defendant-driver was doing 10 mph. Child darts out and driver's car injures him.

The defendant-driver was within the speed limit. He didn't breach the duty; he drove less than 15 mph. Because the plaintiff cannot show a breach of duty, a crucial element in the proof of the defendant's alleged negligence, the analysis or the lawsuit stops here. Since the plaintiff hasn't proved his case, there is nothing for the defendant to defend against. In short, the driver is not negligent and, therefore, not liable to the plaintiff.

To summarize. In example A, there is neither injury nor negligence even though a "duty" has been breached. In example B, there was injury, breach of a duty, proximate cause, negligence, and liability. In example C, there was injury but no breach of duty. The driver was neither negligent nor liable.

Two. The defendant found himself in a situation in which he had sufficient time or information or both to foresee that what he chose to do *could* injure the plaintiff. This criterion is formulated: the defendant knew, or had reason to know, or could foresee that his actions might injure the plaintiff. This criterion's shorthand label is foreseeability.

Facts: Residential area; speed limit 35 mph; children are playing ball on the front lawn; driver doing 35 mph; child darts out after ball and is injured by the car.

What is the duty here? The driver knew, had reason to know, or could foresee that a ball might get away from a child and that some child might very well chase it into the street without looking for oncoming cars. Children can be expected to do just that. When the driver saw children playing ball so close to the street, it was his duty to slow down. He did not and because he didn't, he injured the child. In short, the breach of driver's duty to slow down was the proximate cause of the child's injury. Liability on the basis of negligence follows.

Three. The third criterion is for miscellaneous situations. It is variously formulated: did the defendant use due care? What would a "reasonable man" have done in the same circumstances? Would a "reasonable man" have done what the defendant did? This criterion's shorthand label is the "standard of the reasonable man" or "due care."

No reasonable man would whiz past a school yard full of small children at noontime at 55 mph with or without a traffic sign. Due care on the part of the driver would demand that he slow down regardless of the speed limit when he saw children playing ball near the street. From everyday experiences, one can collect hundreds of situations which indicate clearly what the defendant's duty was.

BREACH of the defendant's duty to plaintiff usually isn't difficult to spell out as long as the duty is clearly spelled out.

PROXIMATE CAUSE means the defendant's breach of duty caused or led directly to the plaintiff's injury. Stated negatively: If it were not for the defendant's breach, or *but for* the defendant's breach, the plaintiff would not have been injured. Like duty, causation must be spelled out in some detail.

INJURY, as mentioned above, is the prerequisite for negligence. Although, in other areas of torts (civil wrongs), what constitutes injury may be the subject of litigation, within the context of medical malpractice, injury is usually clearly seen, often tragic, and easily spelled out.

Procedurally, at trial, the plaintiff must spell out the defendant's duty and demonstrate a breach of that duty, and show an injury, and forge a chain of causation from the breach to the injury that satisfies the judge before the defendant is forced to defend himself. In legal terminology, the plaintiff must present a prima facie case of negligence in order to cast onto the defendant's shoulders the burden of going forward with the evidence (to defend himself). Stated somewhat more practically: unless the plaintiff proves each and every element of negligence, his case cannot be considered by the jury (he cannot get his case to the jury).

Defenses

Once the physician-defendant has the burden of going forward with the evidence, he has several categories of defenses. One. The physician-defendant can challenge the duty that the plaintiff is alleging on several grounds. (a) The duty as spelled out by the plaintiff doesn't apply. (b) The physician can show that, although he didn't follow plaintiff's alleged duty, he followed another duty (therapeutic regimen) that a respectable minority of physicians follow. Here, the physician would also probably have either to show that he didn't cause the injury or show what did cause the injury. (c) The physician can show that, even in the face of good care (when following an acceptable "duty," as articulated by either the plaintiff or defendant) a certain percentage of patients can be expected to develop or sustain the result, complication, or "injury" the plaintiff did. For example, the inexorable march of the patient's disease caused the plaintiff's "injury," not the physician. Here, the physician challenges not only the breach of duty but also the plaintiff's theory of causation.

Two. The physician-defendant can offer a defense that challenges the plaintiff's allegation of what constituted a breach of the duty. Such a challenge is based upon each case's unique fact situation. In addition, the physician challenges the patient's allegation of breach of duty, by implication, when he challenges the plaintiff's articulation of duty.

Three. The physician-defendant can challenge the plaintiff's theory of causation of the injury in several ways. (a) He can prove the plaintiff's theory is wrong. Tactically, the physician-defendant is better advised to show also, if he's able, what did cause the patient's injury. (b) The physician can show the alleged injury was inevitable, was a natural consequence of the plaintiff's disease process, or that the injury was caused by something or someone else for whom he was not responsible.

Four. Malpractice defendants, lawyers and physicians, have one defense available to them that other negligence defendants don't. The courts recognize that often in crucial situations lawyers and physicians can do no more than exercise their best judgment. For this reason, if the physician can convince the court that he exercised his best judgment in the care of his patient, he is not held liable for the patient's injury. This defense is the legal recognition of two facts; one, physicians are not infallible, and two, since the human body has nearly infinite variations, honest judgments can be wrong and cause injury. Only good records can document the physician's best judgment.

Obviously, the best-judgment defense is not open to the physician whose judgment was poor. From the plaintiff's point of view, the physician's poor judgment itself may be negligence, and therefore the cause of the patient's injury.

Five. Under certain narrow conditions, the physician can use a defense of contributory negligence. Usually the fact situation is one in which the physician has adequately and appropriately instructed the patient to do or not to do something as part of the physician's treatment regimen; the patient has not followed those instructions to his detriment; and, it is this detriment — injury — for which the patient is suing the physician for malpractice. In essence the defendant physician is really alleging the patient was negligent by saying, "Patient, you caused the injury yourself."

In some states, contributory negligence is a complete defense and defeats the plaintiff's case. In those states that have the comparative negligence rule, the defendant may be assessed some fraction of the damages, e.g., 35 percent.

Finally, the physician-defendant can allege and prove the plaintiff brought his suit after the Statute of Limitations has run, and, therefore, the plaintiff is barred from bringing his suit.

Statutes of limitations, by setting time limits after which lawsuits cannot be begun, prevent the plaintiff from gaining unfair advantage by suing on stale claims (by not promptly enforcing his rights). The statutes don't say there is no negligence, malpractice, or breach of contract. What they say is that the remedy, the right to bring a lawsuit, is no longer available to the plaintiff. Furthermore, it is unfair to force the defendant to defend an event that took place several years before, because he will not only be unable to recall details of the event, but he will also be unable to amass and marshall his defenses. Records that would ordinarily be kept for defense are mislaid, lost, thrown away, or otherwise destroyed in the natural course of events. Witnesses move away or die; their memories fade and fail.

Each state has enacted its own Statute of Limitations for negligence. In some states, this statute applies to medical malpractice; in others, there is a special statute for medical malpractice.

Certain events toll (stop) the running of the Statute of Limitations. It is tolled until the patient knows or has reason to know he has sustained an injury that might have been caused by the physician's negligence. It is also tolled if the physician fraudulently withholds information about the potentially negligently caused injury, and until the plaintiff-patient knows or has reason to know the true facts of his case. In the case of minors, the Statute may be tolled until they attain their majority.

Records

Whatever the merits of the case, legible, complete, precise, and accurate records are the physician's best bulwark against an allegation of malpractice. From the medical point of view, the patient's history, physical examination, progress notes, laboratory data, and consultants' notes and opinions are the bases upon which the attending physician makes his diagnosis. They are also the bases upon which he plans, evaluates, and modifies his patient's therapeutic regimen. The physician needs no reminding that the patient's clinical record is a mechanism for recording and storing information, communicating information to and from consultants, and it serves as a memory aid to the attending physician. One criterion for how useful a patient's clinical record is: when read at a later date, does its completeness and precision portray an accurate picture of the patient's status at the time it was written?

Legally, the patient's clinical chart is a contemporaneous recording of data and opinion that is made in the normal course of the physician's care of the patient. Because it is contemporaneously made, the clinical record is likely to be both accurate and untainted by memory lapses. Because the patient's record is made for the benefit of the patient and the physician, it is likely to be a true and honest description of the situation at the time it was written. And because the clinical chart is relevant, contemporaneously recorded, untainted by memory lapses, and honestly written, it is considered to be good evidence and usually can be admitted into evidence without difficulty.

Human nature being what it is, a jury is likely to conclude that a sloppy record means sloppy medical care. They are also likely to conclude that an incomplete or cryptic record probably means the physician didn't have all the information necessary and probably went off half-cocked to the detriment (injury) of the patient.

Now, where the physician has amassed and recorded the patient's pertinent medical data, made a diagnosis, explained why he picked that one from his differential diagnostic possibilities, selected a therapeutic regimen, explained his reason for choosing it, and followed the patient, he probably has clearly brought to his care of the patient the training, skill, expertise, and diligence that are demanded of him.

In retrospect, good records may show the physician was in fact negligent for any number of reasons. Physicians are not infallible; they make mistakes; they unintentionally and negligently injure patients. Remember that negligence is an unintentional injuring. It is for these reasons physicians carry malpractice insurance to recompense the injured patient for the damage he has suffered.

Even though the patient's clinical record shows that the physician was negligent or didn't use his best judgment, this is neither a warrant nor an excuse for poor record keeping. It's a warrant for better medical care.

A final remark: the patient's clinical record is not the place for criticizing another physician's care of the patient, editorializing, flip remarks, and medical one-upsmanship. Such entries benefit the writer's ego but not the patient's care or the writer's chances of successfully defending himself.

Function of the Jury and Expert Testimony

Because of their highly technical nature, medical malpractice cases require expert testimony. The jury has the various tasks of establishing the facts of the case before them, of applying the law of the case as given to them by the judge's charge to them, and of deciding the case either for or against the plaintiff. There can be no maybe, perhaps, or let's wait a while; inability to reach a yes or no answer is called a hung jury and entitles the suing party to a new trial.

In order to establish the facts, the jury assesses the credibility of the witnesses and the authenticity of documents. It also has to resolve conflicting testimony by accepting or rejecting one side's version of the case or synthesizing, from both versions, what it thinks really happened. The jury as a unit is considered to have a large pool of information that it can use to resolve disputes arising in the community in which it sits. However, in medical malpractice cases, the jury must decide medical questions of fact that are beyond its common fund of information. Expert testimony is needed to educate or instruct both the judge and jury, and for the jury to decide medical questions of fact. Generally, without medical expert testimony, the plaintiff cannot get his medical malpractice case to the jury.

In theory, although an expert witness is presented by one side or the other, he is supposed to be both neutral and objective. To put it cold-bloodedly, unless the expert advances the cause of the side that presents him, he won't be put on the stand. The more blatantly partisan the expert sounds or acts, the less credible he appears to judge and jury.

Legal v. Medical Causation

Ironically, the jury is occasionally called upon to decide questions for which medical science has no answer. *Menarde v. Philadelphia Transportation Co.*, 376 Pa. 497, 103 A.2d 681 (1954), illustrates this and other points about expert testimony. First, expert medical testimony is needed in many personal injury cases. Second, the question before the jury was one of causation: will or did a single injury cause cancer?

Third, for the physician, the *Menarde* case makes clear the difference between *medical* causation and *legal* causation.

Fourth, *Menarde* raises the important general question of whom the court accepts as an expert witness, specifically here for the causation of cancer. Physicians generally feel they know what the qualifications of a medical expert are and who is a medical expert. Is a general practitioner in Philadelphia an expert on the cause of breast cancer? Is the director of a breast cancer clinic in an oncologic hospital an expert on the cause of cancer of the breast?

Fifth, paragraph [1,2] demonstrates how precedent works. In prior cases which they quote, the Supreme Court of Pennsylvania set forth that quantum of competent evidence they expect the plaintiff to present to the trial court to satisfy it that the plaintiff has met his burden of proof of causation. In the following paragraphs, the Supreme Court applies these rules of law (called "the law of the case") and comes to a conclusion.

Finally, the reader is to read the case critically to see whether or not the court followed its own rules!

How to Read a Case Report

For those reading an appellate case report for the first time, it is helpful to have some idea of its purpose and form. Its purpose is to settle the law — to state clearly what the law is in the area under discussion. These cases state precedents.

Generally, one justice writes the decision or opinion of the court and others concur. Those disagreeing can write a dissenting opinion. Usually, the writer outlines the pertinent facts of the case, states what the issue(s) of law under dispute is, and then proceeds to discuss at greater or lesser length those competing rules of law bearing on the issue, and arrives at a decision. If there are no precedents, the writer discusses the merits of the fact situation from a philosophical or public policy point of view and arrives at a new precedent. The latter is often called one of first impression. The reader should also closely watch the jurist's choice of words for an insight into the jurist's bias or equanimity.

Appellate courts decide issues of law only. With the exception of Louisiana, appellate courts do not make findings of fact — that is for the jury.

If, after the verdict has been rendered, one side or the other (in a trial before the court that hears all the evidence in the case for the first time) feels the trial judge has made one or more *errors of law* which has denied him a fair trial, that party appeals. The appellate court hears the arguments on the legal issue involved and renders a decision. If the appellate court decides no error has occurred, it affirms the lower court's decision. If an error of law has occurred but the court decides the error has not prejudiced the rights of the parties, the court can also affirm the verdict of the lower court. If the appellate court decides prejudicial error has occurred, the case can be remanded for a new trial.

If there is a two-tiered system of appellate courts (a superior and a supreme court) the supreme court can affirm or reverse the lower appellate court's decision. Where weighty questions of law are at stake, the appeal from the trial court's ruling can be certified directly to the highest appellate court.

An appellate court's application of the law chosen to the fact situation is said to be the holding of the case — the precedent set by the case.

MENARDE v. PHILADELPHIA TRANSPORTATION Co.
376 Pa. 497, 103 A.2d 681 (1954)

OPINION BY MR. JUSTICE CHIDSEY, MARCH 22, 1954:

On the morning of May 16, 1949 the plaintiff was injured while alighting from a street car of the defendant. The accident occurred due to the premature starting of the trolley car which caused plaintiff to fall forward into the street. Treatment for injuries to her left ankle, right knee and both hands was administered at Mt. Sinai Hospital; these being the only injuries perceptible at that time. Her family physician, Dr. Martin J. Koebert, attended her in the early evening of the same day to alleviate any remaining pain or shock.

Upon disrobing later that evening for the first time following the accident, plaintiff noticed a discoloration on her right side, including her breast. She recalled Dr. Koebert the following day because the bruised right breast had grown slightly darker over night. He examined the breast and observed the discoloration but having discovered no nodules or lumps, he was not overly concerned and merely prescribed the application of hot compresses to the bruised area. For the first month or two following the accident Dr. Koebert made periodic examinations of the breast and sometime within that interval the discoloration disappeared and the breast seemed perfectly normal and remained so for two months. At the end of July or the beginning of August plaintiff detected a lump on her breast at the exact spot where there was discoloration previously.

She was referred to Dr. Sidney Beck, a cancer specialist, who recommended and performed a radical mastectomy, which entailed the removal of the entire breast and the underlying muscles and the tissues in the arm pit.

. . .

The principal point urged on appeal is that plaintiff failed to meet her burden of establishing by legally competent evidence a causal connection between the accident and the cancer which later developed.

[1,2] In order to link her impaired physical condition to the defendant's conduct, the plaintiff was forced to depend on expert medical testimony because scientific knowledge was required for the elucidation of the question. Having selected experts to speak in her behalf, it has been held essential that no absolute contradictions appear in their ultimate conclusions, although minor points of difference between such witnesses would not necessarily exclude their testimony. [Citation omitted.] Moreover the expert has to testify, not that the condition of claimant might have, or even probably did, come from the accident, but that in his professional opinion the result in question came from the cause alleged. A less direct expression of opinion falls below the required standard of proof and does not constitute legally competent evidence. [Citations omitted.]

[3] Applying these tests to the present case, in our opinion the medical testimony offered in support of the claim met the required standard and was not so contradictory that the finding of the jury was predicated upon speculation. Dr. Koebert, who was associated with the plaintiff's case from the time of the accident, testified on direct examination that in his opinion the injury was the direct cause of the cancer, and the salient portions of his testimony on cross-examination are as follows: "Q. Could there possibly have been something else which contributed to this cancer? A. I do not think we are able to say. Q. Can we say that this particular bruising or injury, to the exclusion of everything else, caused this cancer? A. I believe other conditions which had happened, and according to the highlights of the case as I examined her originally, and in that it arose in

that immediate area, I believe that this cancer was caused directly by the injury. Q. Is it not possible that something else contributed to it? A. Within the knowledge of man, I think not. . . . Q. Would you say that it is impossible that there was any other thing that could have caused this cancer other than the blow? A. In this case I would say not."

On redirect examination he was asked: "Q. Doctor, is there even the slightest idea of speculation in your mind as to the judgment you have come to in concluding that this accident caused this cancer in this girl's body? A. I believe that this accident was the direct cause of this woman's cancer. Q. And is that judgment based on any speculation whatsoever in this case? A. Not in this case, no."

Dr. Beck, the other expert called by the plaintiff, was in charge of the breast cancer clinic at the American Oncologic Hospital in Philadelphia. Basing his ultimate conclusion on certain accepted criteria, which he asserts were present in this case, he testified that he must conclude that the trauma sustained in this accident caused the cancer. While it may be said that his testimony was characterized by some indefiniteness or uncertainty, such testimony pertained principally to the cause of cancer in general and the disparity of opinion which exists among outstanding authorities in this field as to whether a single trauma can produce cancer. Where, as here, a person who has enjoyed prior good health sustains an injury to a particular member and some three months thereafter a malignant nodule appears in precisely the same location as the bruise, and two doctors conclude that the cancer resulted from the trauma, causal connection between the accident and the disease is sufficiently established. [Citation omitted.]

• • •

The defendant presented no medical expert testimony on the causation of cancer. The plaintiff won her case in the trial court and was successful on appeal.

The "certain accepted criteria" Dr. Beck used are proposed by Ewing. They are the criteria for the cause of cancer by a single trauma: (a) an injury; (b) a tumor must appear at the site of injury, (i) within a reasonable time span from injury to the appearance of the tumor, and (ii) the tumor must be of that tissue where injury occurred, (not metastatic).

Do criteria used by an eminent cancer specialist fulfill the Pennsylvania Supreme Court's own criteria for causation?

Is Good Medicine Good Law?

The physician would think that good medicine is good law. 'Tain't so. In many, many cases, good medicine is accepted by the courts as the duty that the physician should follow. However, there is a small number of cases in which the physician is surprised to find himself held negligent when he has followed what was in fact a nearly universally followed medical standard. *Helling v. Carey*, 83 Wash. 2d 514, 519 P.2d 981 (1974), was just such a case.

The medically unsettling case of *Helling v. Carey*, which follows, is an illustration of how the courts set the physician's duty.

HELLING v. CAREY
83 Wash. 2d 514, 519 P.2d 981 (1974)

HUNTER, J. — This case arises from a malpractice action instituted by the plaintiff (petitioner), Barbara Helling.

The plaintiff suffers from primary open angle glaucoma. Primary open angle glaucoma is essentially a condition of the eye in which there is an interference in the ease with which the nourishing fluids can flow out of the eye. Such a condition results in pressure gradually rising above the normal level to such an extent that damage is produced to the optic nerve and its fibers with resultant loss in vision. The first loss usually occurs in the periphery of the field of vision. The disease usually has few symptoms and, in the absence of a pressure test, is often undetected until the damage has become extensive and irreversible.

The defendants (respondents), Dr. Thomas F. Carey and Dr. Robert C. Laughlin, are partners who practice the medical specialty of ophthalmology. Ophthalmology involves the diagnosis and treatment of defects and diseases of the eye.

The plaintiff first consulted the defendants for myopia,

nearsightedness, in 1959. At that time she was fitted with contact lenses. She next consulted the defendants in September 1963, concerning irritation caused by the contact lenses. Additional consultations occurred in October 1963; February 1967; September 1967; October 1967; May 1968; July 1968; August 1968; September 1968; and October 1968. Until the October 1968 consultation, the defendants considered the plaintiff's visual problems to be related solely to complications associated with her contact lenses. On that occasion, the defendant, Dr. Carey, tested the plaintiff's eye pressure and field of vision for the first time. This test indicated that the plaintiff had glaucoma. The plaintiff, who was then 32 years of age, had essentially lost her peripheral vision and her central vision was reduced to approximately 5 degrees vertical by 10 degrees horizontal.

Thereafter, in August of 1969, after consulting other physicians, the plaintiff filed a complaint against the defendants alleging, among other things, that she sustained severe and permanent damage to her eyes as a proximate result of the defendants' negligence. During trial, the testimony of the medical experts for both the plaintiff and the defendants established that the standards of the profession for that specialty in the same or similar circumstances do not require routine pressure tests for glaucoma upon patients under 40 years of age. The reason the pressure test for glaucoma is not given as a regular practice to patients under the age of 40 is that the disease rarely occurs in this age group. Testimony indicated, however, that the standards of the profession do require pressure tests if the patient's complaints and symptoms reveal to the physician that glaucoma should be suspected.

The trial court entered judgment for the defendants following a defense verdict. The plaintiff thereupon appealed to the Court of Appeals, which affirmed the judgment of the trial court. [Citation omitted.] The plaintiff then petitioned this court for review, which we granted.

• • •

. . . The issue is whether the defendants' compliance with the standard of the profession of ophthalmology, which does not require the giving of a routine pressure test to persons under 40 years of age, should insulate them from liability under the facts in this case where the plaintiff has lost a substantial amount of her vision due to the failure of the defendants to timely give the pressure test to the plaintiff.

The defendants argue that the standard of the profession, which does not require the giving of a routine pressure test to persons under the age of 40, is adequate to insulate the defendants from liability for negligence because the risk of glaucoma is so rare in this age group. The testimony of the defendant, Dr. Carey, however, is revealing as follows:

> Q. Now, when was it, actually, the first time any complaint was made to you by her of any field or visual field problem? A. Really, the first time that she really complained of a visual field problem was the August 30th date. [1968] Q. And how soon before the diagnosis was that? A. That was 30 days. We made it on October 1st. Q. And in your opinion, how long, as you now have the whole history and analysis and the diagnosis, how long had she had this glaucoma? A. I would think she probably had it ten years or longer. Q. Now, Doctor, there's been some reference to the matter of taking pressure checks of persons over 40. What is the incidence of glaucoma, the statistics, with persons under 40? A. In the instance of glaucoma under the age of 40, is less than 100 to one per cent. The younger you get, the less the incidence. It is thought to be in the neighborhood of one in 25,000 people or less. Q. How about the incidence of glaucoma in people over 40? A. Incidence of glaucoma over 40 gets into the two to three per cent category, and hence, that's where there is this great big difference and that's why the standards around the world has been to check pressures from 40 on.

The incidence of glaucoma in one out of 25,000 persons under the age of 40 may appear quite minimal. However, that one person, the plaintiff in this instance, is entitled to the same protection, as afforded persons over 40, essential for timely detection of the evidence of glaucoma where it can be arrested to avoid the grave and devastating result of this disease. The test is a simple pressure test, relatively inexpensive. There is no judgment factor involved, and there is no doubt that by giving the test the evidence of glaucoma can be detected. The giving of the test is harmless if the physical condition of the eye permits. The testimony indicates that although the condition of the plaintiff's eyes might have at times prevented the defendants from administering the pressure test, there is an absence of evidence in the record that the test could not have been timely given.

Justice Holmes stated in *Texas & P. Ry. v. Behymer*, 189 U.S. 468, 470, 47 L.Ed. 905, 23 S.Ct. 622 (1903):

> What usually is done may be evidence of what ought to be done, but what ought to be done is fixed by a standard of reasonable prudence, whether it usually is complied with or not.

In *The T.J. Hooper*, 60 F.2d 737 (2d Cir. 1932), Justice Hand stated on page 740:

> [I]n most cases reasonable prudence is in fact common prudence; but strictly it is never its measure; a whole calling may have unduly lagged in the adoption of new and available devices. It never may set its own tests, however persuasive be its usages. *Courts must in the end say what is required; there are precautions so imperative that even their universal disregard will not excuse their omission.*

(Italics added.)

Under the facts of this case reasonable prudence required the timely giving of the pressure test to this plaintiff. The precaution of giving this test to detect the incidence of glaucoma to patients under 40 years of age is so imperative that irrespective of its disregard by the standards of the ophthalmology profession, it is the duty of the courts to say what is required to protect patients under 40 from the damaging results of glaucoma.

We therefore hold, as a matter of law, that the reasonable standard that should have been followed under the undisputed facts of this case was the timely giving of this simple, harmless pressure test to this plaintiff and that, in failing to do so, the defendants were negligent, which proximately resulted in the blindness sustained by the plaintiff for which the defendants are liable.

• • •

The judgment of the trial court and the decision of the Court of Appeals is reversed, and the case is remanded for a new trial on the issue of damages only.

HALE, C. J., and ROSELLINI, STAFFORD, WRIGHT and BRACHTENBACH, JJ., concur.

UTTER, J. (concurring) — I concur in the result reached by the majority. I believe a greater duty of care could be imposed on the defendants than was established by their profession. The duty could be imposed when a disease, such as glaucoma, can be detected by a simple, well-known harmless test whose results are definitive and the disease can be successfully arrested by early detection, but where the effects of the disease are irreversible if undetected over a substantial period of time.

The difficulty with this approach is that we as judges, by using a negligence analysis, seem to be imposing a stigma of moral blame upon the doctors who, in this case, used all the precautions commonly prescribed by their profession in diagnosis and treatment. Lacking their training in this highly sophisticated profession, it seems illogical for this court to say they failed to exercise a reasonable standard of care. It seems to me we are, in reality, imposing liability, because, in choosing between an innocent plaintiff and a doctor, who acted reasonably according to his specialty but who could have prevented the full effects of this disease by administering a simple, harmless test and treatment, the plaintiff should not have to bear the risk of loss. As such, imposition of liability approaches that of strict liability.

Strict liability or liability without fault is not new to the law. Historically, it predates our concepts of fault or moral responsibility as a basis of the remedy. Wigmore, *Responsibility for Tortious Acts: Its History*, 7 Harv. L. Rev. 315, 383, 441 (1894). As noted in W. Prosser, *The Law of Torts* § 74 (3d ed. 1964) at pages 507, 508:

> There are many situations in which a careful person
> is held liable for an entirely reasonable mistake. . . . in
> some cases the defendant may be held liable,
> although he is not only charged with no moral
> wrongdoing, but has not even departed in any way
> from a reasonable standard of intent or care. . . .
> There is "a strong and growing tendency, where there
> is blame on neither side, to ask, in view of the exigen-
> cies of social justice, who can best bear the loss and
> hence to shift the loss by creating liability where
> there has been no fault."

(Footnote omitted.) Tort law has continually been in a
state of flux. It is "not always neat and orderly. But this is
not to say it is illogical. Its central logic is the logic that
moves from premises — its objectives — that are only partly
consistent, to conclusions — its rules — that serve each
objective as well as may be while serving others too. It is
the logic of maximizing service and minimizing disservice
to multiple objectives." Keeton, *Is There a Place for Negligence in Modern Tort Law?*, 53 Va. L. Rev. 886, 897
(1967).

When types of problems rather than numbers of cases
are examined, strict liability is applied more often than
negligence as a principle which determines liability. Peck,
Negligence and Liability Without Fault in Tort Law, 46
Wash. L. Rev. 225, 239 (1971). There are many similarities
in this case to other cases of strict liability. Problems of
proof have been a common feature in situations where
strict liability is applied. Where events are not matters of
common experience, a juror's ability to comprehend
whether reasonable care has been followed diminishes.
There are few areas as difficult for jurors to intelligently
comprehend as the intricate questions of proof and standards in medical malpractice cases.

In applying strict liability there are many situations
where it is imposed for conduct which can be defined with
sufficient precision to insure that application of a strict
liability principle will not produce miscarriages of justice
in a substantial number of cases. If the activity involved is
one which can be defined with sufficient precision, that
definition can serve as an accounting unit to which the

costs of the activity may be allocated with some certainty and precision. With this possible, strict liability serves a compensatory function in situations where the defendant is, through the use of insurance, the financially more responsible person. Peck, *Negligence and Liability Without Fault in Tort Law, supra* at 240–241.

If the standard of a reasonably prudent specialist is, in fact, inadequate to offer reasonable protection to the plaintiff, then liability can be imposed without fault. To do so under the narrow facts of this case does not offend my sense of justice. The pressure test to measure intraocular pressure with the Schiotz tonometer and the Goldman applanometer takes a short time, involves no damage to the patient, and consists of placing the instrument against the eyeball. An abnormally high pressure requires other tests which would either confirm or deny the existence of glaucoma. It is generally believed that from 5 to 10 years of detectable increased pressure must exist before there is permanent damage to the optic nerves.

Although the incidence of glaucoma in the age range of the plaintiff is approximately one in 25,000, this alone should not be enough to deny her a claim. Where its presence can be detected by a simple, well-known harmless test, where the results of the test are definitive, where the disease can be successfully arrested by early detection and where its effects are irreversible if undetected over a substantial period of time, liability should be imposed upon defendants even though they did not violate the standard existing within the profession of ophthalmology.

· · ·

FINLEY and HAMILTON, JJ., concur with UTTER, J.

Law of the Rescuer

In the course of his career, the physician will come upon emergency situations outside the hospital and his office. If the physician has not caused the emergency situation, was not a party to an automobile accident, for instance, he has no legal duty to act. But if he undertakes to care for the injured, he has assumed the duty to act reasonably. The law of the rescuer is reasonably well settled: if a person who is under no duty to aid someone who is injured or in peril voluntarily acts to aid the victim, the volunteer assumes the duty to use reasonable care. If the volunteer does not act reasonably and the injured person is made worse, the volunteer is held liable.

Good Samaritans (volunteers) have been held liable to the victim if the volunteer's actions worsened the victim's condition by (1) increasing the danger, (2) leading the victim to believe the danger was past, when it was not, or (3) inducing the victim to forgo help from others. (Annot., 64 A.L.R.2d 1181).

The burgeoning spate of medical malpractice suits has made physicians disinclined to voluntarily come to the aid of injured victims in an emergency situation such as an auto accident. To induce physicians to voluntarily care for the injured at the scene of the emergency, some states have enacted Good Samaritan statutes that, with the exception of gross negligence, excuse a physician who gives emergency care at the scene from civil liability (Annot., 39 A.L.R.3d 222). These statutes have not had sufficient constitutional challenges or statutory constructions to say more. As might be suspected, in the drafting of such a statute, it is quite difficult to include only those situations one wishes to include without at the same time embracing wider or unwanted situations. At this point, it is a good exercise in legal drafting for the reader to try to draft a Good Samaritan statute.

Additional Reading

Atiyah, quoted by O'Connell, J. and Henderson, R. C. *Tort Law, No-Fault and Beyond.* New York: Matthew Bender, 1975. pp. 684–695.

Malone, W. S. Ruminations on the role of fault in the history of torts. *The Origin and Development of the Negligence Action.* U.S. Dept. of Transportation, Automobile Insurance and Compensation Study, 1970. U.S. Government Printing Office.

Prosser, W. L. *Handbook of the Law of Torts,* 4th ed. St. Paul: West Publishing Co., 1971.

Quimby, C. W., Jr. and Spies, F. K. *Liability of the Hospital Cardiac Arrest Team.* 26 Arkansas Law Review (1972):17.

Traynor, R. *The Ways and Meanings of Defective Products and Strict Liability.* 32 Tennessee Law Review (1965):363.

Wildavsky, A. No Risk is the Highest Risk of All. *American Scientist* 67 (1979):32–37.

Chapter
Three

Consent and
Informed Consent

III

The two sections of this chapter cover two closely related, legally sensitive areas of the patient-physician relationship: consent and informed consent.

Consent has a long tradition based on the fundamental Anglo-American principle of law that the individual shall be the sole arbiter of who shall and who shall not touch him. Because consent involves a basic individual freedom, the courts jealously guard that right and severely punish those who interfere with it.

Informed consent is a new and developing area of the law of negligence, whose rules of law are less precise than those of consent. The doctrine of informed consent requires the physician to inform his patient about a proposed procedure so the patient is equipped to participate in making decisions about his or her own medical treatment.

Consent

Consent rests on the fundamental principle of the freedom and dignity of the individual that no one shall touch the body of a person without that person's consent.

An unlawful touching of a person is a battery; an assault is an offer of a battery with the immediate capability of doing so. Once the defendant touches the assaulted person, it is a battery.

Assault and battery may be either a civil or a criminal offense. When its occurrence is likely to threaten the peace and quiet of the community, it is treated as a criminal offense by fine, imprisonment, or both.

As a civil offense, assault and battery falls within the category of an intentional tort. (1) Even though the defendant's unlawful touching doesn't injure the plaintiff, the defendant still has to pay money damages, nominal though they may be, for the interference with a fundamental right. (2) If the plaintiff suffers injury, the defendant is liable in money damages for that injury. (3) If the defendant's behavior is outrageous, he will have to pay, in addition to damages, punitive damages. Note that civil assault and battery has kept some of its criminal flavor.

The gist of the plaintiff's complaint is the invasion of his basic right to bodily integrity, which the courts zealously guard. Procedurally, all the plaintiff has to show is an unconsented-to touching. That's all! An injury only affects the magnitude of the money damages the defendant is forced to pay the plaintiff. Should the physician operate without the patient's consent, neither the good result of the treatment nor the fact that the patient's injury was a known, non-negligently caused result will be heard in the physician's defense. Those defenses are irrelevant and immaterial.

Medical care is replete with the physician's touching the patient. Every time the physician does an examination, he doesn't ask permission to touch the patient. Only on certain occasions is consent necessary. Consent can be given in one of three ways. The patient can give his written or oral consent to something the physician intends to do. The patient can give consent by his behavior. For example, the physician can reasonably believe the patient has given his consent when, after the physician says, "I'd like to listen to your heart," the patient takes off his shirt and bares his chest.

Consent may also arise by the operation of a legal fiction. For example, *implied consent* arises under the following circumstances. A patient is brought to the emergency room badly injured and unconscious; he requires an immediate operation; and the physicians operate on him successfully. At some later date, the courts will not hear the patient complain that the physicians performed the emergency operation on him without his consent (battered him). Because the law presumes each person wishes to continue to live, the law conclusively presumes the patient would have given consent, were he able.

In obtaining consent from the patient, some practical questions arise for the physician. When to get written permission? To what did the patient consent? Who can give consent? Unfortunately, these questions have no hard and fast answers.

One. By tradition, written consents seem to be obtained when the proposed diagnostic or therapeutic procedure carries some risk or danger to the patient, or when the patient's body is to be invaded. These seem reasonable rules to follow.

Two. To what has the patient consented? More precisely phrased: did the patient understand to what he was giving consent? Since the patient may have understood one thing and the physician another, it is advisable for the physician to get a witnessed, signed consent which clearly sets forth what he plans to do. Although no hard and fast rules exist for the contents of a consent, a journalistically complete recording of *what* is to be done to the patient by *whom, when,* and *where* would seem to be adequate. *Why* and *how* can be specified too, but *why* should be found in the patient's clinical record, and *how* will appear in the operative report.

The utility of the written, witnessed, and signed consent is that, should a legal dispute over consent arise in the future, a contemporaneously executed memorandum has reduced the intentions and understandings of the parties to writing for the court to read.

Three. A person who has reached the age of majority and who is legally and mentally competent can give his own consent. Each state has a statute defining the age of majority, which the physician ought to consult. From here things get hazy.

Parents can give consent for their children. In the absence of parents, the child's legal guardian can. It sometimes gets sticky when the parents are unavailable and no legal guardian has been appointed. The best course here is for the physician to try to find the parents and document that effort. If necessary, the court can appoint a guardian to give the requisite permission before the necessary elective surgery. If an emergency exists, the physician can proceed on that basis and appropriately document that fact.

Sticky questions about minors arise. Can minors give their consent to treatment for venereal disease or obtain an abortion without their parents' knowledge or consent? Some states have settled this question by statute. The best thing for the physician to do is get legal advice from attorneys practicing in his state.

Some states extend to emancipated minors several rights of those who have reached their majority. One of these rights is to give consent for medical treatment. An emancipated minor is one who is not living with his parents and who is supporting himself adequately. It extends to married minors who have established their own households.

Generally, where a husband or wife is unable to give consent, the spouse can. Divorce represents no problem in consent; the divorced ex-spouse cannot give consent. The area of separation is hazy.

Mohr v. Williams, 95 Minn. 261, 104 N.W. 12 (1905), which follows, illustrates a number of points about consent. It is a case of first impression; the Supreme Court of Minnesota had not ruled on the particular question before. Apparently, from its comment, few other courts at that time had. Hence, the Minnesota Supreme Court had to analyze the fact situation using fundamental principles of law and arrive at a decision, which would then be precedent for other similar cases in the state.

Another point is that the court differentiates criminal and civil assault and battery. Note that in a suit for assault and battery expert testimony is not needed! Even if the patient gets a good result from the operation to which he or she did not give consent, the patient can collect damages. The plaintiff's contention is that "My bodily integrity was invaded without my consent. Therefore, since our society zealously guards my individual freedom to say who shall touch me, punish the defendant by making him pay money damages rather than imprisonment, because he did not do it with evil intent."

The opinion is somewhat difficult to read and slow going because of the involved sentences and the liberal use of the passive voice. The style is legal-eaglese. Ignore the procedural matters.

Mohr v. Williams
95 Minn. 261, 104 N.W. 12 (1905)

Brown, J. [footnote omitted]

Defendant is a physician and surgeon of standing and character, making disorders of the ear a specialty, and having an extensive practice in the city of St. Paul. He was consulted by plaintiff, who complained to him of trouble with her right ear, and, at her request, made an examination of that organ for the purpose of ascertaining its condition. He also at the same time examined her left ear, but, owing to foreign substances therein, was unable to make a full and complete diagnosis at that time. The examination of her right ear disclosed a large perforation in the lower portion of the drum membrane, and a large polyp in the middle ear, which indicated that some of the small bones of the middle ear (ossicles) were probably diseased. He informed plaintiff of the result of his examination, and advised an operation for the purpose of removing the polyp and diseased ossicles. After consultation with her family physician, and one or two further consultations with defendant, plaintiff decided to submit to the proposed operation. She was not informed that her left ear was in any way diseased, and understood that the necessity for an operation applied to her right ear only. She repaired to the hospital, and was placed under the influence of anaesthetics; and, after being made unconscious, defendant made a thorough examination of her left ear, and found it in a more serious condition than her right one. A small perforation was discovered high up in the drum membrane, hooded, and with granulated edges, and the bone of the inner wall of the middle ear was diseased and dead. He called this discovery to the attention of Dr. Davis — plaintiff's family physician, who attended the operation at her request — who also examined the ear and confirmed defendant in his diagnosis. Defendant also further examined the right ear, and found its condition less serious than expected, and finally concluded that the left, instead of the right, should be operated upon; devoting to the right ear other treatment. He then performed the operation of ossiculectomy on plaintiff's left ear; removing a portion of the drum membrane, and scraping away the diseased portion of the inner wall of the ear. The operation was in every way successful and skilfully performed. It is claimed by plaintiff that the operation greatly impaired her hearing, seriously injured her person, and, not having been consented to by her, was wrongful and unlawful, constituting an assault and battery; and she brought this action to recover damages therefor.

· · ·

2. We come then to a consideration of the questions presented by defendant's appeal from the order denying his motion for judgment notwithstanding the verdict. It is contended that final judgment should be ordered in his favor for the following reasons: (a) That it appears from the evidence received on the trial that plaintiff consented to the operation on her left ear. (b) If the court shall find that no such consent was given, that, under the circumstances disclosed by the record, no consent was necessary. (c) That, under the facts disclosed, an action for assault and battery will not lie; it appearing conclusively, as counsel urge, that

there is a total lack of evidence showing or tending to show malice or an evil intent on the part of defendant, or that the operation was negligently performed.

We shall consider first the question whether, under the circumstances shown in the record, the consent of plaintiff to the operation was necessary. If, under the particular facts of this case, such consent was unnecessary, no recovery can be had, for the evidence fairly shows that the operation complained of was skilfully performed and of a generally beneficial nature. But if the consent of plaintiff was necessary, then the further questions presented become important. This particular question is new in this state. At least, no case has been called to our attention wherein it has been discussed or decided, and very few cases are cited from other courts. We have given it very deliberate consideration, and are unable to concur with counsel for defendant in their contention that the consent of plaintiff was unnecessary.

The evidence tends to show that, upon the first examination of plaintiff, defendant pronounced the left ear in good condition, and that, at the time plaintiff repaired to the hospital to submit to the operation of her right ear, she was under the impression that no difficulty existed as to the left. In fact, she testified that she had not previously experienced any trouble with that organ. It cannot be doubted that ordinarily the patient must be consulted, and his consent given, before a physician may operate upon him.

It was said in the case of Pratt v. Davis, 37 Chicago Leg. News, 213, referred to and commented on in 60 Cent. Law J. 452: "Under a free government, at least, the free citizen's first and greatest right, which underlies all others — the right to the inviolability of his person; in other words the right to himself — is the subject of universal acquiescence, and this right necessarily forbids a physician or surgeon, however skilful or eminent, who has been asked to examine, diagnose, advise, and prescribe (which are at least necessary first steps in treatment and care), to violate, without permission, the bodily integrity of his patient by a major or capital operation, placing him under an anaesthetic for that purpose, and operating upon him without his consent or knowledge."

1 Kinkead Torts, § 375, states the general rule on this subject as follows: "The patient must be the final arbiter as to whether he shall take his chances with the operation, or take his chances of living without it. Such is the natural right of the individual, which the law recognizes as a legal right. Consent, therefore, of an individual, must be either expressly or impliedly given before a surgeon may have the right to operate." There is logic in the principle thus stated, for, in all other trades, professions, or occupations, contracts are entered into by the mutual agreement of the interested parties, and are required to be performed in accordance with their letter and spirit. No reason occurs to us why the same rule should not apply between physician and patient. If the physician advises his patient to submit to a particular operation, and the patient weighs the dangers and risks incident to its performance, and finally consents, he thereby, in effect, enters into a contract authorizing his physician to operate to the extent of the consent given, but no further.

It is not, however, contended by defendant that under ordinary circumstances consent is unnecessary, but that, under the particular circumstances of this case, consent was implied; that it was an emergency case, such as to authorize the operation without express consent or permission. The medical profession has made signal progress in solving the problems of health and disease, and they may justly point with pride to the advancements made in supplementing nature and correcting deformities, and relieving pain and suffering. The physician impliedly contracts that he possesses, and will exercise in the treatment of patients, skill and learning, and that he will exercise reasonable care and exert his best judgment to bring about favorable results. The methods of treament are committed almost exclusively to his judgment, but we are aware of no rule or principle of law which would extend to him free license respecting surgical operations. Reasonable latitude must, however, be allowed the physician in a particular case; and we would not lay down any rule which would unreasonably interfere with the exercise of his discretion, or prevent him from taking such measures as his judgment dictated for the welfare of the patient in a case of emergency. If a person should be injured to the extent of rendering him unconscious, and his injuries were of such a nature as to require prompt surgical attention, a physician called to attend him would be justified in applying such medical or surgical treatment as might reasonably be necessary for the preservation of his life or limb, and consent on the part of the injured person would be implied. And again, if, in the course of an operation to which the patient consented, the physician should discover conditions not anticipated before the operation was commenced, and which, if not removed, would endanger the life or health of the patient, he would, though no express consent was obtained or given, be justified in extending the operation to remove and overcome them.

But such is not the case at bar. The diseased condition of plaintiff's left ear was not discovered in the course of an operation on the right, which was authorized, but upon an independent examination of that organ, made after the authorized operation was found unnecessary. Nor is the evidence such as to justify the court in holding, as a matter of law, that it was such an affection as would result immediately in the serious injury of plaintiff, or such an emergency as to justify proceeding without her consent. She had experienced no particular difficulty with that ear, and the questions as to when its diseased condition would become alarming or fatal, and whether there was an immediate necessity for an operation, were, under the evidence, questions of fact for the jury.

3. The contention of defendant that the operation was consented to by plaintiff is not sustained by the evidence. At least, the evidence was such as to take the question to the jury. This contention is based upon the fact that she was represented on the occasion in question by her family physician; that the condition of her left ear was made known to him, and the propriety of an operation thereon suggested, to which he made no objection. It is urged that by his conduct he assented to it, and that plaintiff was bound thereby. It is not claimed that he gave his express consent. It is not disputed but that the family physician of plaintiff was present on the occasion of the operation, and at her request. But the purpose of his presence was not that

he might participate in the operation, nor does it appear that he was authorized to consent to any change in the one originally proposed to be made. Plaintiff was naturally nervous and fearful of the consequences of being placed under anaesthetics, and the presence of her family physician was requested under the impression that it would allay and calm her fears. The evidence made the question one of fact for the jury to determine.

4. The last contention of defendant is that the act complained of did not amount to an assault and battery. This is based upon the theory that, as plaintiff's left ear was in fact diseased, in a condition dangerous and threatening to her health, the operation was necessary, and, having been skilfully performed at a time when plaintiff had requested a like operation on the other ear, the charge of assault and battery cannot be sustained; that, in view of these conditions, and the claim that there was no negligence on the part of defendant, and an entire absence of any evidence tending to show an evil intent, the court should say, as a matter of law, that no assault and battery was committed, even though she did not consent to the operation. In other words, that the absence of a showing that defendant was actuated by a wrongful intent, or guilty of negligence, relieves the act of defendant from the charge of an unlawful assault and battery.

We are unable to reach that conclusion, though the contention is not without merit. It would seem to follow from what has been said on the other features of the case that the act of defendant amounted at least to a technical assault and battery. If the operation was performed without plaintiff's consent, and the circumstances were not such as to justify its performance without, it was wrongful; and, if it was wrongful, it was unlawful. As remarked in 1 Jaggard, Torts, 437, every person has a right to complete immunity of his person from physical interference of others, except in so far as contact may be necessary under the general doctrine of privilege; and any unlawful or unauthorized touching of the person of another, except it be in the spirit of pleasantry, constitutes an assault and battery. In the case at bar, as we have already seen, the question whether defendant's act in performing the operation upon plaintiff was authorized was a question for the jury to determine. If it was unauthorized, then it was, within what we have said, unlawful. It was a violent assault, not a mere pleasantry; and, even though no negligence is shown, it was wrongful and unlawful. The case is unlike a criminal prosecution for assault and battery, for there an unlawful intent must be shown. But that rule does not apply to a civil action , to maintain which it is sufficient to show that the assault complained of was wrongful and unlawful or the result of negligence. [Citations omitted.]

• • •

The *Mohr* case stands for the legal proposition that the physician must scrupulously respect the right of the patient to specify exactly what the physician can and cannot operate on. Without legal perspective, it is incomprehensible to the physician that the patient in *Mohr* should be awakened from anesthesia, allowed to recover sufficiently to give her undrugged consent to operate on the more diseased ear, and then be subjected, a second time, to the dangers of induction and emergence from anesthesia, when the whole thing could have been done the first time. Legally, this argument is irrelevant and immaterial.

The patient's consent was clear. The courts cannot and will not permit anyone to modify or disregard a person's exercise of his fundamental right to say who shall touch him. You can see the court's point. If they had let the operating surgeon get consent for one thing and then let him do something else, how long do you think this fundamental right would last?

Mohr doesn't address itself to the question: Could Mrs. Mohr's husband have given consent? That question must await another lawsuit.

Informed Consent

Development of the Doctrine

The doctrine of informed consent is the legal analysis and evaluation of what the physician told the patient in order to obtain his consent for a proposed diagnostic or therapeutic procedure. This developing legal doctrine arose in response to a legally perceived wrong which resulted from advances in medical practice. As the number, complexity, and danger of diagnostic and therapeutic procedures increased, courts began to see more and more patients who sustained complications (injuries). In these cases, the injured plaintiff alleged negligence, but there was none. So, an innocently injured plaintiff went unrecompensed — a wrong without a remedy.

Although the injured plaintiff could have alleged that the physician fraudulently obtained his consent (by withholding information, slanting it, or outright lying), fraud is hard to prove in court and physicians don't generally obtain consent fraudulently. Furthermore, since fraud is mainly a problem in contracts, and since the consent to a medical procedure is not currently intellectually fashionably viewed as signing a contract for the procedure, the legal theories of breach of contract and fraud aren't open to the plaintiff.

Social Bases of the Doctrine

About the same time as the above cases appeared, patient attitudes toward their physicians began to change. Patients today feel they are better educated than their forebears, and astute enough in medical matters because of media coverage, to participate in the decisions regarding their care. Although physicians are likely to dispute this thesis, patients, nevertheless, want more say in the medical decisions that affect them.

Viewed contemporaneously, and couched in terms of consumerism, informed consent is the shorthand term for the legal analysis of the following question: has the physician (supplier of services) supplied the patient (consumer) with sufficient data or information to arrive at a decision to give or withhold consent to a proposed diagnostic procedure or therapeutic regimen? More succinctly, did the physician hoodwink the patient into buying the procedure? Note the flavor of truth-in-lending; the lender must disclose hidden charges and total costs to the borrower.

Legal Premises

To the nonlawyer, the aim of informed consent is likely to be unclear, its rules of law lacking definition, and its rationale hazy. Its aim is to encourage the physician to inform his patient so that he is equipped to participate in making decisions about his medical care and treatment. The rules of informed consent lack definition because they have not been honed by centuries of refinement.

To the lawyer, the rationale of informed consent is clear, almost second nature, and represents a way of thinking. In these cases, an un-articulated premise is that the patient-physician relationship is basically unequal. The inequality stems from both the physician's superior knowledge of medicine and the patient's need, often urgent, for care without the ability to bargain for it. By training, a lawyer's perception of an unequal relationship brings to mind a body of law with which he is familiar, the law of the fiduciary.[1]

Over the centuries, the law has had extensive experience with un-equal relationships. In the area of contracts, the law looks with favor upon *full disclosure* between the parties and with disfavor upon *fraud*—one party setting up an unequal relationship. In the areas of the guardian and incompetent, the trustee and beneficiary of a trust, the executor or administrator and heirs or legatees, the law has long since found these relationships to be basically unequal.

Fiduciaries (guardians, trustees, executors, administrators), as a class, have great power over both the well-being of and the property designated for the benefit of someone who has a legal disability (minority or insanity). Because of his disability, the beneficiary of the property is unable to protect his interest in that property against the fiduciary. Without the courts, the beneficiary must rely on the fiduciary. To protect the benficiary from an over-reaching fiduciary, the courts have developed a large body of law spelling out in detail what the fiduciary can and cannot do. If, in the eyes of the law, the fiduciary breaches his trust, his punishment is both severe and fitting—he loses considerable standing both financially and professionally.

There is little doubt that the physician has great power over the life and well-being of the patient who must rely on and trust him. These are the necessary elements of a fiduciary relationship. Viewed in this light, the law easily sees and analyzes the patient-physician relationship in the traditional terms of the fiduciary. This is a relationship the courts feel impelled to oversee.

Seeing the physician as a fiduciary, at this stage of the doctrine of informed consent's development, the courts advise the physician to disclose fully to his patients: (1) the benefits of the proposed pro-

---

[1]See *Tunkl,* pp. 71, 72ff.

cedure; (2) its risks; (3) the expected outcome of the patient's disease without treatment; and, (4) alternative forms of diagnosis or therapy.

As far as risks of the procedure are concerned, the courts suggest the patient is primarily interested in four areas. Risk of death due to the procedure, problems of recuperation, disability, and the chances of disfigurement from the procedure.

The Remedy

The courts, in order to adjust the common law to current social values and to fashion a remedy for a perceived but unrecompensed, unintentional wrong, have either found or imposed an affirmative duty of the physician to inform the patient. Once the affirmative duty was articulated, the traditional negligence analysis followed: breach of a duty that leads directly to an injury is our old friend, negligence, liability, and money damages.

To the physician, informed consent sounds the death knell of that aspect of the patient-physician relationship wherein the physician said, "Do as I say and everything'll be all right," and the patient acquiesced, "Yes, Doctor." That's out!

Viewed strictly from the standpoint of negligence: the physician owed a duty to his patient to disclose the risks of the procedure to him; the physician did not tell the patient of a procedure's known risk or complication (injury); that particular complication occurred in the absence of the physician's negligence. The patient alleges, "I would not have consented to this operation had I been informed of this complication. Therefore, because the physician breached his duty by failing to inform me of this complication, which did occur, I have been injured. Since I have sustained an injury due to the physician's breach of his duty to me, I demand money damages."

There are two lines of cases on the need for expert witnesses. One line holds expert testimony is not necessary. All the patient must do is *show* he was not told of a risk or complication and that risk occurred and *state*, "Had I known of the risk that eventuated I wouldn't have consented to the operation." Note that the plaintiff doesn't allege that the physician performed the procedure negligently.

The other line of cases requires the patient to produce other physicians, expert witnesses, from the same or similar communities who will testify that it is good medical practice to tell the patient of that particular risk, which the defendant-physician didn't do.

Pitfalls for the Physician

The physician must be extremely careful in his choice of language to the patient for two reasons. First, the courts expect the physician to use language which he thinks the patient will understand. Second, the physician must couch his disclosures to the patient in terms that do not so alarm the patient that he refuses needed treatment. At this point we come to a legal and philosophic junction. If, by legal fiat, the patient must be given the information based upon the above criteria, then the law must expect some patients to be frightened. However, in future decisions, the law will have to balance the risk of frightening some patients against the benefits of full disclosure to all patients. Although this point has not been clearly answered, consistency with the underlying rules and principles of the patient's right to know and right to control who touches him (consent) would seem to point to the conclusion that the law will force the occasional patient to bear the risk of being frightened.

It is clear at this point that we are dealing with what and how accurately the patient remembers and comprehends the information that the physician told him prior to anesthesia and surgery or other procedure (before the complication). Within such a psychiatrically, psychologically, and semantically slippery area, the potential physician-defendant can only protect himself against a future charge of lack of informed consent both by giving the patient those facts demanded by the law and by outlining what he told the patient *in the patient's chart*. The details of the physician written record will depend upon three factors: (1) facts of the case; (2) magnitude of the procedure; and (3) how completely and how concisely the physician records the information.

When the patient wishes to and does receive an explanation, the physician can outline in the patient's chart what he told the patient, how much the patient understood, and that the patient's consent was obtained. This is about all the physician can do.

Some patients may not wish to be burdened with this information and so tell their physician. Obviously, the physician is not expected to pursue the point and is excused from presenting the information prior to obtaining consent. In order to document the patient's preference not to know, a short note to that effect in the patient's clinical chart would seem adequate.

A problem arises for the physician when he feels the patient's mental status is such that informing him would be detrimental to his best interests. There is no clear answer to this question from the courts yet.

Again, the physician should record on the patient's chart, in clear terms, his reasons for not informing the patient prior to obtaining the consent for the procedure or operation. The decisions in this area clearly signal that these cases are likely to be the rare exception and wholesale resort to this defense will not be tolerated.

In addition to the physician's note, it would seem to be good sense for the physician not only to discuss the reasons for not informing the patient but also to explain to a responsible member of the family the risks, benefits, alternative treatments, and expected outcome if the procedure is not done.

Presenting the frequency of morbidity and mortality (risk) to the patient is also a slippery task for the physician. How far down the list of complications, arranged according to decreasing frequency, should he go? There is no answer to this numbers game and there is not likely to be. But common sense would lead the physician to inform his patient of the risks of death, disability, disfigurement, difficulties in recuperation, and, after that, those risks which in the best judgment of the physician fairly represent the risk of injury to his patient.

Finally, it must be clearly understood that a properly signed and witnessed consent form for the proposed procedure says nothing about *informed* consent. All the signed consent form says is that the patient has given written consent to the proposed procedure. Whether the physician supplied sufficient information so that the patient could make that decision has to be resolved in court, should the patient care to contest the sufficiency of the given information.

If informed consent demonstrates nothing else to the physician, it makes clear that, in a developing area of the law, the rules of law are likely to lack definition, and their slow development on a case-by-case basis will inevitably lead to some bad decisions where some innocent defendants will be held liable. It is to be hoped that the number of poor decisions will be held to a minimum. Instead of waiting for the arduous case-by-case honing of the rules of informed consent, state legislatures could pre-empt the area of informed consent and enact a statute answering many, at present, unanswered questions.

Chapter
Four

Contracts

IV

This chapter has several purposes: first, to explore what a contract is, how one is made, and what the contract terms are; second, to examine the patient-physician contract; and third, to explain how others can make the physician an unwitting party to a contract. Finally, the entire chapter can be considered a transition from the professional side of medical practice to its business side.

Most people are acquainted with written or printed contracts with all their "whereases," "to wits," and fine print. However, most people don't realize they enter into and fulfill many unwritten contracts daily without ever being aware the contracts exist. This is as it should be. Any contract that sees the inside of a courtroom means that somewhere between its formation and execution, the parties or their respective attorneys have failed in their duties.

Sufficient contracts have been made, fulfilled, broken, and litigated over the centuries so that legal scholars have been able to compile and put down in concise form the rules of contract law. Reduction to concise rules doesn't mean the law of contracts is cut and dried. Far from it. Human frailty being what it is, the diversity of subject matter of a contract and the almost infinite variety of situations in which contracts can arise preclude the law of contracts from ever being cut and dried. But what such compilations of rules means is that a large body of contract law exists which is available to guide the behavior of those persons who contemplate entering into a contract. Skillfully used, this body of law will keep contract disputes to a minimum. What the physician knows about contracts and when to seek advice about them will help keep him in his office and out of the courtroom.

Rules of Law

Traditionally, rules of contract law (and other areas of the law) have been distilled from thousands of case reports (printed court decisions). From time to time, legal writers, scholars, and legal groups have compiled their rules in one or several volumes with more or less extensive comments. In the United States, the Restatement of the Law of Contracts is one compilation that was published some 45 to 50 years ago by the American Law Institute (ALI). It is currently undergoing a revision, and will be known as the Restatement (Second) of the Law of Contracts. Some sections of black-letter law (so-called because the rules are printed in heavy black type) from the proposed Second Restatement are used to sum up some of the important elements of the law of contracts.

From the very outset, the reader must understand that these black-letter rules of law are extremely high level abstractions. They are intended to cover, and have been distilled from, contracts dealing with an almost infinite variety of subject matter and arising from widely differing situations. The application of these highly abstract rules of law to specific fact situations, for example, two or more people fighting over a particular contract, is what makes the study and practice of law fascinating to attorneys.

A Simple Contract

Perhaps the oldest, simplest, and easiest contract to dissect and understand is: a housewife goes to a farmers' market, sees a cabbage she wants to buy for a price she is willing to pay, picks up the cabbage and, at the same time, hands the farmer the money for the cabbage, which he accepts, and walks away with her cabbage.

Even though not a word was spoken and no written document was drawn up, agreed to, and witnessed, this fact situation has all the basic elements of a contract. First, by piling his cabbages with their prices marked on them (the subject matter of a potential contract) in the farmers' market, the cabbage farmer can be said to have made an *offer* to sell them. Section 24 of the proposed Second Restatement of Contracts defines an offer:

> An offer is the manifestation of willingness to enter into a bargain, so made as to justify another person in understanding that his assent to that bargain is invited and will conclude it.

Note the mercantile or commercial flavor of the language. By use of the word "bargain" for "contract," one can almost hear the haggling over the price in the bazaar. Haggling or the opportunity to haggle over price is the basic idea of a contract.

Second, the *terms* of the offer are (1) the clearly marked price on each cabbage (more specifically, the price marked on the cabbage she picked up); and (2) that both the housewife and farmer knew the price was to be paid in cash at the time of the sale.

Third, the housewife's handing over the price (money) to the farmer, who accepted it, was her *acceptance* of his offer to sell the cabbage. Section 52(1) defines the acceptance of an offer:

> Acceptance of an offer is a manifestation of assent to the terms thereof made by the offeree in a manner invited or required by the offer.

Fourth, when the housewife walked away with the cabbage, she showed that the bargain (contract) had been concluded. (See § 24).

Practically, this contract has been made and carried out, fulfilled, or, technically, executed. Everyone is happy with it. It is not at all likely this contract will ever see the inside of a courtroom.

Warranty

But, let us suppose that housewife and her family developed food poisoning from the cabbage. What then? Since the relationship between housewife, her family, and cabbage farmer rests on the cabbage contract, she and her family will sue the cabbage farmer for damages on the basis of that contract.

Cabbage farmer's defense would run, in part, as follows: "Yes, I sold you the cabbage, but no term of the contract mentioned, alluded to, or implied anything about food poisoning from eating the cabbage."

Housewife and family would counter this argument by showing that cabbages sold in the farmers' market are meant to be eaten. The court would accept this counterargument, commenting that the farmer knew this and impliedly (not expressly) warranted (promised or guaranteed) that the cabbages that he offered for sale were fit to eat.

Since housewife's cabbage was not fit to eat, cabbage farmer had breached the judicially added warranty that it was fit to eat. As a result, the court ordered cabbage farmer to pay damages to housewife and family to remedy the injury the breach of contract caused them.

In essence, the judge has written into the cabbage contract a term for the parties. This written-in term is called an implied warranty. Here, the warranty says that the subject matter of the contract is fit for the purpose or use intended. Concisely, this is an implied warranty of merchantability.

A party to a contract can warrant something orally or in writing. Such a contract term is called an express warranty.

Reasonable Price

Let us suppose the cabbage farmer had not marked a price on any of the cabbages and housewife walked up to them, took one, and walked away with it. This could be stealing; but if farmer hauled housewife into criminal court, she'd go to jail for stealing, and he'd lose both his cabbage and its price.

On the other hand, cabbage farmer could allege a contract and its breach under the following sections of the proposed Second Restatement:

  1. A contract is a promise or a set of promises for the breach of which the law gives a remedy, or the performance of which the law in some way recognizes as a duty.
  5. A promise may be stated in words either oral or written, or may be inferred wholly or partly from conduct.
  228(1). Words and other conduct are interpreted in the light of all the circumstances, and if the principal purpose of the parties is ascertainable, it is given great weight.

The practical problems of proof would be difficult. Without a written contract, oral testimony with all its disadvantages is the only way to show the offer and its terms, acceptance, the subject matter of the contract (which may have long since disappeared into cole slaw or sauerkraut), and the circumstances surrounding the contract. This is why in complex transactions written contracts are not only useful but also, in certain circumstances, mandatory. Furthermore, it is easier to try the case.

Housewife might try to defend on the ground that the cabbages were offered for the taking because there was no price on any of them. (See §§ 24 and 52(1).) The cabbage farmer and the judge could easily cut through this defense by showing that the farmers' market wasn't a give-away depot and, furthermore, she knew or had reason to know the cabbages were for sale. The conflict would then narrow down to the crucial issue; what was the price of the cabbage? To this the cabbage farmer would say that all he wanted was a "reasonable price" for his cabbage. To this the judge would blandly reply, "Prove to this court's satisfaction what a reasonable price is and we shall order the housewife to pay it."

How much simpler all this would have been if cabbage farmer had only marked the price on his cabbages. In effect, the court has written in for the parties a crucial term of their contract, exact price.

Consideration

There is another element of a contract that is technically important but will be covered only briefly for our purposes — consideration. For our purposes, consideration can be seen in the following formation of a service contract: Your lawn needs cutting; a young man knocks on your door and says, "Your lawn needs cutting. I'll cut it for you."

You say, "Go ahead."

He cuts the lawn.

There is little doubt that a bargain has been struck. Your promise to pay can be found to arise from § 5, how a promise may be made.

A promise may be stated in words either oral or written, or may be inferred wholly or partly from conduct.

And, under § 228(1) Rules in Aid of Interpretation:

Words and other conduct are interpreted in the light of all the circumstances, and if the principal purpose of the parties is ascertainable, it is given great weight.

In consideration of your promise to pay the young man, he either promised to cut your lawn or actually cut it. *Consideration* is not only that which is paid for the promise but also that which convinces the courts that you should be forced to keep, or carry out, or be bound by your promise to pay him the reasonable value of his services.

The terms of the contract are reasonably complete and definite even though they are not expressly spelled out. To determine the exact amount of the reasonable value of the young man's services may require a lawsuit.

This analysis of the lawn-cutting contract makes the proposed Second Restatement's definition of a contract somewhat easier to grasp. Section 1 defines a contract as follows:

> A contract is a promise or a set of promises for the breach of which the law gives a remedy, or the performance of which the law in some way recognizes as a duty.

In a service contract, the implied warranty analogous to merchantability is that the work will be carried out or done in a workmanlike manner.

Patient-Physician Contract

What has all this got to do with the patient-physician contract? The physician doesn't cut grass or sell something tangible, like cabbages. That's true. What he sells are intangibles: his time, medical training, skill, experience, ability, and expertise. In other words, the physician sells his services, medical care. The patient buys the physician's medical care with the expectation that it will cure him.

Let us examine more closely the contractual aspects of the patient-physician relationship between newly licensed general practitioner and his first patient. Just after town's newest physician finishes hanging his license on his office wall and hanging out his shingle, Mr. Jones spots the shingle and decides to see why he's losing weight, is so thirsty all the time, and has to void so often, both day and night. The physician ushers Mr. Jones into the office, asks what's troubling him, listens to his chief complaints, takes a complete history, does a physical examination, has his office nurse perform the appropriate laboratory tests, diagnoses diabetes mellitus, and sets up a program for its management that includes several return visits. At the end of the month, the physician sends Mr. Jones an itemized bill for his services:

initial examination, subsequent visits, and the costs of the laboratory tests. The patient feels better, is satisfied with his care, and pays the bill.

Technically, the physician's shingle can be considered an invitation to negotiate for medical care. In line with the freedom to contract with whomever one wishes, a physician is not obligated to accept each person who applies to him for medical care. In other words, the physician has the right to refuse to treat or care for a person. However, once the physician does accept the person as a patient (establishes the patient-physician relationship), then certain legal obligations arise on both sides.

A legal analysis would run as follows: by taking Mr. Jones as his patient and prominently displaying his license on his office wall, the physician has "held himself out" as a physician, *offered* medical care for sale.

By going to the physician, giving his chief complaints and history, submitting to a physical examination, cooperating with the nurse in obtaining the necessary specimens, and returning for follow-up visits, Mr. Jones *accepted* the physician's offer of medical care. (See § 52(1).

Using the same facts, a promise to pay the reasonable cost or price of medical care can be found. (See § 5, how a promise may be made.)

Fees

It would have been better business for the physician to have discussed fees (price) with Mr. Jones. This would have obviated any dispute about how much the physician charged. Had "reasonable fees" been litigated, what the physician received would have been equal to or less than what was billed, but not more.

The courts, in hearing physicians' contract cases to collect fees, feel that the patient-physician contract hasn't been arrived at by arm's length dealings. The purchase of the cabbage and cutting of the lawn contracts were arrived at by an arm's length transaction. Housewife could have bought her cabbage from some other farmer, or none at all, if she chose. Cabbage farmer didn't have to sell to her if she didn't meet his price. The young man was under no pressure to offer to cut the lawn; you could have said, "No, thank you." Both transactions are said to have been arrived at or negotiated at arm's length. Neither party to the contract was at a disadvantage to the other.

Courts feel that the ill patient is at a disadvantage because, by the very fact the patient needs medical care, he is unable to shop around, bargain, or haggle to get the best price (fee). The upshot of all this is that the physician should frankly and openly discuss fees with his patients beforehand. By doing so, the courts feel the patient is placed in a less disadvantaged position.

Warranty

Suppose the patient refuses to pay his bill. His side of the argument is: "I went to the physician expecting him to cure me. He didn't. I've still got diabetes. He broke the contract. I'm not going to pay." Suppose, further, the physician's attorney decides to sue to collect the physician's fees.

The rub here is the patient's expectations. The question is, who engendered these expectations, the patient or the physician, and how?

First, let us assume the physician did not promise, guarantee, or warrant any cure; the expectation came from the patient. From a highly technical analysis, there was no offer of a cure from the physician. Hence, there was nothing to accept. Put somewhat less technically, in ascertaining the principal purpose of the parties, the courts dislike hidden meanings, wishes, and unarticulated expectations. Since the courts don't like guessing games, they aren't likely to find a promise to cure.

Furthermore, over the centuries the courts have amassed a pretty good working knowledge of what medicine can and cannot do. They know the physician neither offers nor intends to offer a cure. They know that what he does offer is the careful and diligent application of his medical skills to the care of the patient. Through their decisions over the years, the courts have incorporated this "careful, diligent application of medical skills" term into the patient-physician contract. This term limits or defines what the patient can reasonably expect from the physician. Alternatively, it defines what society expects of the physician.

Second, let us assume the physician did promise the patient a cure. Because the physician has full liberty to do so, the physician will be held to that promise. Just what he promised or led the patient to expect will have to be shown by written evidence or, more probably, by oral testimony.

Third, let us assume the physician playfully, jokingly, or in an attempt to support or encourage the patient, said to him, "You'll be as good as new." More than likely, the patient will *interpret* this as a promise. Herein lies the rub. Since that was the promise the patient wanted to hear, he took the physician's offhand remark, not in the manner it was meant, but uncritically and at face value.

There are several good medical reasons why the physician can expect a patient to interpret the offhand remark as a promise. The patient is usually frightened and concerned about his symptoms, their meaning, and what might happen to him. In addition, the patient consults the physician not only for treatment but also for support and encouragement. Finally, the patient wants to get better. All this is human nature. These are further reasons why the patient-physician contract is not an arm's length transaction.

After treatment when the patient is not as good as new, he is naturally upset, disappointed, frustrated, and angry. All this time, he'd been led to believe he'd be as good as new and he isn't. The disgruntled patient may take out his frustrations by suing the physician for malpractice, by just not paying his bill, or by suing for breach of contract.

There is little doubt that a judge or jury will easily conclude that the physician did make a promise or guarantee to the patient. Recall § 1 of the proposed Second Restatement of the Law of Contracts. "A contract is a promise...for the breach of which the law gives a remedy...."

"The physician didn't make me as good as new; therefore, the physician has breached his contract with me," says the patient. What are the patient's remedies for breach of contract? The patient doesn't have to pay his bill because he didn't get what he bargained for. The patient can sue the physician for damages whose magnitude will have to be worked out in court.

There are three points to remember here. One, the physician is under no obligation to guarantee or promise the patient anything. If he does so, he does it at his peril. Two, since the patient coming to the physician for medical care is psychologically vulnerable, he is likely to take what the physician says uncritically, at face value, or interpret it as he wishes. Three, it behooves the physician to be extremely careful in what he says to the patient about the efficacy of the proposed treatment, lest the physician guarantee or promise the patient something unintentionally. (Recall § 228(1).) Obviously, no surgeon will promise his operative patient that he won't have a scar. No plastic surgeon will promise a patient that he will be either satisfied or beautiful afterwards.

This discussion is not intended to imply that, to protect themselves, physicians ought to draw up written contracts for the care of their patients. But if, in selected cases, a physician does feel that such a contract is needed, then the best course of action is to get the advice and services of an attorney to advise him and draft whatever document is indicated.

Case Reports

The following case, *Guilmet v. Campbell*, 385 Mich. 57, 188 N.W.2d 601, 43 A.L.R.3d 1194 (1971), emphasizes how careful the physician must be when discussing a proposed course of treatment with a patient.

The legal issue was: did Dr. Campbell's discussion with the plaintiff-patient before the operation constitute or rise to the level of an offer to or a promise to achieve a specific result? Furthermore, did the plaintiff-patient enter into the contract (consent to surgery) for the gastric operation because of or in reliance on this promise to achieve a specific result? This is another way of asking, did the offeree accept the offer?

Four additional points. One, this decision makes reference to rules of procedure. Legal procedural rules are similar to rules of order for deliberative bodies and exist for the same reasons: to conduct an orderly trial. A "motion for a judgment notwithstanding the jury's verdict" or "judgment n.o.v." is an example of a procedural device. Since procedure is not essential to us, ignore it.

Two, the decision points out that this is a tough case to decide because, whether the Supreme Court decides for plaintiff or for defendant, the resulting precedent will have a profound, lasting, and unfortunate effect on future cases brought in the state. What the judges are saying is, whichever way this case is decided, the precedent will be bad. By implication, they are saying, this precedent is likely to be restricted to the narrow fact situation outlined in this case. This is summed up in a legal aphorism: tough cases make bad law.

Three, notice how skillfully the plaintiff's attorney elicited the answers from his client which were necessary for the elements of a contract: offer and what its terms were; acceptance; the plaintiff-patient had the operation. Did the defendants fulfill the contract; in other words, did the plaintiff-patient get what he bargained for?

Four, notice also that the court puts great emphasis on the defendants' inducing the plaintiff's reliance on their prior discussion. "...the observations and descriptions of the result which the defendant made were promises to achieve that specific end, and were *inducements* upon which plaintiff...*relied* in proceeding with the operation." (See pages 68–70; emphasis added.) In contract cases, if the court can find one party inducing another party to rely on the first party's inducements, an enforceable contract will nearly always be found.

GUILMET v. CAMPBELL

385 Mich. 57, 188 N.W.2d 601, 43 A.L.R.3d 1194 (1971)

T. G. KAVANAGH, J. — This appeal presents a very simple question but it is fraught with great danger to the public weal.

The question is: Was the trial court in error in refusing to grant defendant's motion for a judgment notwithstanding the jury's verdict for the plaintiffs?

The defendants are skilled surgeons who performed a relatively complicated operation on plaintiff Richard Guilmet, and after such operation the plaintiffs suffered very great damages.

The danger attendant upon decision here is that on one hand if we sanction the award of damages to the plaintiffs we may foster suits which threaten the freedom physicians and surgeons must have in the practice of their vital profession, and on the other hand if we deprive these plaintiffs of their award, we not only may do them an injustice but impair the very process by which we seek to administer justice.

The facts and circumstances giving rise to the suit are as follows:

In the fall of 1963 the plaintiff had suffered near fatal bleeding through a peptic ulcer. At that time he was being treated by Dr. Klewicki and it was Dr. Klewicki who recommended the defendant surgeons. In January of 1964 the plaintiff went to see the surgeon "***curious about an operation, if I should have one or if I shouldn't have one***." It was never indicated to the plaintiff that he *must* have the operation.

Defendant Dr. Campbell testified that prior to the operation the plaintiff was in excellent physical condition and the operation was *not* an emergency.

At the first consultation with the defendant, Dr. Campbell, the following conversation took place according to the plaintiff's testimony:

Q. Now what was the nature of the conversation? Did you state your purpose in being there?

A. Yes, I asked Dr. Campbell—I was curious about an operation, if I should have one or if I shouldn't have one, I told him. He knew of my records. I started to tell him about my records. He said, 'I know all about your records.' I said, 'Fine.' He told me, he said, *'Once you have an operation, it takes care of all of your troubles,'* and he said, *'You can eat as you want to, you can drink as you want to, you can go as you please.'*

Q. This type of operation we are talking about then is a stomach or an ulcer operation, is that right?

A. Yes, it is.

Q. Did you talk with him at all about his familiarity with this type of operation or the extent of the operation?

A. Yes, I did.

Q. What was the conversation as you recall it?

A. Well, he explained to me how they do this operation, and at that time he told me that him and his associate, Dr. Arena, were specialists, *and there was nothing to it at all. It was a very simple operation according to them.*

Q. Did he talk at all about whether he had performed these before?

A. Yes, he did.

Q. And what was the conversation along those lines?

A. I asked him how often. He said, *'Very often.'*

Q. Any discussion as to complications or problems that may arise, that may result?

A. I asked him about it, how long I'd be out of work. He said, 'Approximately *three to four weeks at the most,'* and I asked him about any complications, anything dangerous. He said, *'No, there is no danger at all in this operation.'*

Q. Was there any discussion as to where it would take place, how long you'd be convalescing in the hospital?

A. He said 'Beaumont Hospital.' I'd probably be in four to five days and *then I'd be off work maybe another two to three weeks.*

Q. You say he was familiar with your background. Was he aware that you were taking various medications, Maalox and things of this nature?

A. Yes, he was.

Q. You had been taking these pills for a number of months, had you not?

A. Yes, I had.

Q. What was the discussion about the future use of medication?

A. Well, he said, *'after this operation, you can throw your pillbox away, your Maalox you can throw away,'* and then he come up with an example.

Q. Give the example.

A. The example was that *'In twenty years if you could figure out what you spent for Maalox pills and doctors calls, you could buy an awful lot. Weigh it against an operation.'*

Q. Was there any conversation with him as to operations he had performed on other individuals who had treated for a while?

A. Yes. He told me, he never mentioned no names. He just told me of a gentleman that he knows treated for an ulcer thirty years and he went in, had this operation, *and he is altogether a different man at this time.*

Q. Now at the time of the conversation were you back to work?

A. Yes, I was.

(Emphasis added.)

Following this conversation the plaintiff Richard Guilmet underwent the operation.

The record contains a stark description of the troubles that thereafter befell him.

The record description of the vagotomy reveals activity around and on the esophagus. On March 4, 1964 the day following the operation Dr. Wood — a specialist in thoracic surgery on the staff of Beaumont Hospital examined plaintiff and diagnosed: "Ruptured esophagus due to surgical trauma in doing the vagotomy with bilateral effusion and mediastinal emphysema and mediastinitis." Dr. Wood testified that the symptoms displayed by the patient would cause him concern, that the mortality rate from a ruptured esophagus is 50% to 75%.

After the original operation plaintiff went through three subsequent operations for the insertion of tubes to drain excess fluid from his body; he suffered hepatitis which the defendant Dr. Campbell thought was probably caused by one of the many pints of blood he had been given; due to plaintiff's constant coughing and vomiting when eating, his weight fell from 170 pounds to 88 pounds and he was unrecognizable; he was unable to sleep due to coughing and only a return to the hospital and insertion of a drainage tube enabled him to sleep; and finally, he is scarred badly from the operations; he is unable to hold down two jobs as he once could; he is physically weak and unable to be athletically or socially active, and Dr. Wood testified that it is not unusual for recurrences of one of his infections as long as 20 years later.

The plaintiffs brought suit for their damages in a two count complaint. One count asserted negligence on the part of the defendants in performing the operation, and the other count charged a breach of contract. . . .

• • •

The jury returned a verdict of "no negligence" on the tort count but awarded the plaintiffs $50,000 on the breach of contract count.

Following this verdict the defendants moved for judgment notwithstanding the verdict, and the trial court denied it.

This decision was affirmed by the Court of Appeals and we granted leave in light of our conviction that it raised questions of the indicated significance to the jurisprudence of this state.

• • •

. . . [The plaintiffs] claim, . . . , that the observations and descriptions of the result which the defendant made were promises to achieve that specific end, and were inducements upon which plaintiff, Richard Guilmet, relied in proceeding with the operation. They characterize it as an undertaking to "cure" him of the stomach disorder from which he was then suffering.

This appellation of "cure" may be unfortunate.

The parties when contracting never used the word "cure" and the mere elimination of a troublesome condition may not always be properly so designated. For example, a headache may be eliminated by decapitation but no one seriously suggests that it is a "cure." Similarly the substitution of a different stomach disorder for a specific one is not properly called a "cure" of the original ailment.

The gravamen of the plaintiffs' breach of contract complaint is that: 1) The following is the gist of what the defendants told him:

"Once you have an operation it takes care of all your troubles. You can eat as you want to, you can drink as you want to, you can go as you please. Dr. Arena and I are specialists, there is nothing to it at all — it's a very simple operation. You'll be out of work three to four weeks at the most. There is no danger at all in this operation. After the operation you can throw away your pill box. In twenty years if you figure out what you spent for Maalox pills and doctor calls, you could buy an awful lot. Weigh it against an operation."

2) That this amounted to an offer of a contract to achieve by the operation the condition described.

3) That in reliance on the description, the plaintiff accepted the offer, and in breach of the contract the condition described did not result.

In effect by their motion for judgment N.O.V., the defendants ask the court to rule as a matter of law that such statements by defendant *before the parties had contracted for the operation* as to the danger, convalescence, and result can *not* be regarded as a term of a contract between a physician and his patient.

This we will not do for we agree with Mr. Justice COOLEY when he said:

"***where the terms of a negotiation are left to oral proofs, the question what the parties said and did, and what they intended should be understood thereby, is single and cannot be separated so as to refer one part to the jury and another part to the judge; but in its entirety the question is one of fact. [Citations omitted]."

. . .

We hold that the terms of a contract, when contested, are for the jury's determination. This is true even when the evidence of the terms is uncontradicted. [Citations omitted.]

. . .

What we are saying is that under some circumstances the trier of fact might conclude that a doctor so speaking did contract to "cure" his patient.

What was said, and the circumstances under which it was said always determines whether there was a contract at all and if so what it was. These matters are always for the determination of the fact finder. . . .

Justice TALBOT SMITH [citation omitted] articulated our concern for the sensitivity of this area of engagement, when he said:

"A doctor and his patient, of course, have the same general liberty to contract with respect to their relationship as other parties entering into consensual relationship with one another, and a breach thereof will give rise to a cause of action. It is proper to note, with respect to the contracts of physicians, that certain qualitative differences should be observed, since the doctor's therapeutic reassurance that his patient will be all right, not to worry, must not be converted into a binding promise by the disappointed or quarrelsome."

This sound counsel, however, should not be read to import a different standard to this relationship than to any other. It merely stresses the importance of circumstances in determining the effect of words in establishing a contract. The qualitative difference between the relationship of a physician and his patient and the relationship between a shopkeeper and his customer is a significant circumstance the fact finder must remember in assaying their respective words of undertaking.

In this case the trial judge instructed the jury in part:

"Now, on the other hand, the two doctors take the position first of all, that they did not enter into a contract to effect a cure or a result, but that they only agreed to perform with such degree of care and knowledge and attention as is ordinarily possessed by practitioners of their profession under like circumstances. In other words, *they say that they did not assure to the plaintiffs any cure or specific result,* * * *". (Emphasis added).

As in all contract cases for personal services, in order to find for the plaintiffs here the jury must have found from the evidence that the doctors made a specific, clear and express promise to cure or effect a specific result which was in the reasonable contemplation of both themselves and the plaintiff which was relied upon by the plaintiff.

The plaintiffs say they did, the defendants say they did not.

We conclude that under the circumstances disclosed by this record the trial court was correct in sending this case to the jury to determine the offer, acceptance, breach and damages, and refusing to grant judgment notwithstanding their verdict.

As did the Court of Appeals, we affirm.

Plaintiffs may tax costs.

T. M. Kavanagh, C. J., and Adams, Swainson, and Williams, JJ., concurred with T. G. Kavanagh, J.

The following case, *Tunkl v. Regents of the University of California*, 60 Cal. 2d 92, 383 P.2d 441, 32 Cal. Rptr. 33 (1963), illustrates several points: first, the reasons why the parties to the contract were unequal in their bargaining power or position, i.e., they cannot be said to have been bargaining at arm's length. Second, the court bases its decision only lightly on the statutory or prior law but heavily on public policy. Third, although this case involves a hospital, the word "physician" could be inserted for "hospital" with the same outcome. Fourth, the opinion can be looked at, on the one hand, as an essay on the rationale for public utility regulation; or, on the other hand, as an essay on why society, through its courts, demands restraint on the part of the one having a superior bargaining position, when he deals with one whose ability to deal with him is limited for whatever reason. Finally, what the following case really says is that the actions of the hospital did not fit the court's ideas of elementary fairness.

TUNKL v. THE REGENTS OF THE UNIVERSITY OF CALIFORNIA
60 Cal. 2d 92, 383 P.2d 441, 32 Cal. Rptr. 33 (1963)

TOBRINER, J. — This case concerns the validity of a release from liability for future negligence imposed as a condition for admission to a charitable research hospital. For the reasons we hereinafter specify, we have concluded that an agreement between a hospital and an entering patient affects the public interest and that, in consequence, the exculpatory provision included within it must be invalid under Civil Code section 1668.

Hugo Tunkl brought this action to recover damages for personal injuries alleged to have resulted from the negligence of two physicians in the employ of the University of California Los Angeles Medical Center, a hospital operated and maintained by the Regents of the University of California as a nonprofit charitable institution. Mr. Tunkl died after suit was brought, and his surviving wife, as executrix, was substituted as plaintiff.

The University of California at Los Angeles Medical Center admitted Tunkl as a patient on June 11, 1956. The Regents maintain the hospital for the primary purpose of aiding and developing a program of research and education in the field of medicine; patients are selected and admitted if the study and treatment of their condition would tend to achieve these purposes. Upon his entry to the hospital, Tunkl signed a document setting forth certain "Conditions of Admission." The crucial condition number six reads as follows: "RELEASE: The hospital is a nonprofit, charitable institution. In consideration of the hospital and allied services to be rendered and the rates charged therefor, the patient or his legal representative agrees to and hereby releases the Regents of the University of California, and the hospital from any and all liability for the negligent or wrongful acts or omissions of its employees, if the hospital has used due care in selecting its employees."

Plaintiff stipulated that the hospital had selected its em-

ployees with due care. The trial court ordered that the issue of the validity of the exculpatory clause be first submitted to the jury and that, if the jury found that the provision
did not bind plaintiff, a second jury try the issue of alleged
malpractice. When, on the preliminary issue, the jury returned a verdict sustaining the validity of the executed release, the court entered judgment in favor of the Regents.
[Footnote omitted.] Plaintiff appeals from the judgment.

• • •

We begin with the dictate of the relevant Civil Code
section 1668. The section states: "All contracts which have
for their object, directly or indirectly, to exempt anyone
from responsibility for his own fraud, or willful injury to
the person or property of another, or violation of law,
whether willful or negligent, are against the policy of the
law."

• • •

. . . The cases have consistently held that the exculpatory
provision may stand only if it does not involve "the public
interest." [Footnote omitted.] Interestingly enough, this
theory found its first expression in a decision which did not
expressly refer to section 1668. In *Stephens* v. *Southern
Pac. Co.* (1895) 109 Cal. 86, [41 *P.* 783, 50 Am. St. Rep.
17, 29 L.R.A. 751], a railroad company had leased land,
which adjoined its depot, to a lessee who had constructed a
warehouse upon it. The lessee covenanted that the railroad
company would not be responsible for damage from fire
"caused from any . . . means." (P. 87.) This exemption, under the court ruling, applied to the lessee's damage
resulting from the railroad company's carelessly burning
dry grass and rubbish. Declaring the contract not "viola-
tive of sound public policy" (p. 89), the court pointed out
". . . As far as this transaction was concerned, the parties
when contracting stood upon common ground, and dealt
with each other as A and B might deal with each other with
reference to any private business undertaking. . . ." (P. 88.)
The court concluded "that the *interests of the public* in the

contract are more sentimental than real" (p. 95; italics added) and that the exculpatory provision was therefore enforceable.

• • •

On the other hand, courts struck down exculpatory clauses as contrary to public policy in the case of a contract to transmit a telegraph message [citation omitted] and in the instance of a contract of bailment [citation omitted]. In *Hiroshima* v. *Bank of Italy* (1926) 78 Cal. App. 362, [248 P. 947], the court invalidated an exemption provision in the form used by a payee in directing a bank to stop payment on a check. The court relied in part upon the fact that "the banking public, as well as the particular individual who may be concerned in the giving of any stop-notice, is interested in seeing that the bank is held accountable for the ordinary and regular performance of its duties, and, also, in seeing that directions in relation to the disposition of funds deposited in ʾ[the] bank are not heedlessly, negligently, and carelessly disobeyed and money paid out, contrary to directions given." (P. 377.) The opinion in *Hiroshima* was approved and followed in *Grisinger* v. *Golden State Bank* (1928) 92 Cal. App. 443, [268 P. 425]. [Footnote omitted.]

If, then, the exculpatory clause which affects the public interest cannot stand, we must ascertain those factors or characteristics which constitute the public interest. The social forces that have led to such characterization are volatile and dynamic. No definition of the concept of public interest can be contained within the four corners of a formula. The concept, always the subject of great debate, has ranged over the whole course of the common law; rather than attempt to prescribe its nature, we can only designate the situations in which it has been applied. We can determine whether the instant contract does or does not manifest the characteristics which have been held to stamp a contract as one affected with a public interest.

[1] In placing particular contracts within or without the category of those affected with a public interest, the courts have revealed a rough outline of that type of transaction in

which exculpatory provisions will be held invalid. Thus the attempted but invalid exemption involves a transaction which exhibits some or all of the following characteristics. It concerns a business of a type generally thought suitable for public regulation. The party seeking exculpation is engaged in performing a service of great importance to the public, which is often a matter of practical necessity for some members of the public. The party holds himself out as willing to perform this service for any member of the public who seeks it, or at least for any member coming within certain established standards. As a result of the essential nature of the service, in the economic setting of the transaction, the party invoking exculpation possesses a decisive advantage of bargaining strength against any member of the public who seeks his services. In exercising a superior bargaining power the party confronts the public with a standardized adhesion contract of exculpation, and makes no provision whereby a purchaser may pay additional reasonable fees and obtain protection against negligence. Finally, as a result of the transaction, the person or property of the purchaser is placed under the control of the seller, subject to the risk of carelessness by the seller or his agents. [Footnotes omitted.]

While obviously no public policy opposes private, voluntary transactions in which one party, for a consideration, agrees to shoulder a risk which the law would otherwise have placed upon the other party, the above circumstances pose a different situation. In this situation the releasing party does not really acquiesce voluntarily in the contractual shifting of the risk, nor can we be reasonably certain that he receives an adequate consideration for the transfer. Since the service is one which each member of the public, presently or potentially, may find essential to him, he faces, despite his economic inability to do so, the prospect of a compulsory assumption of the risk of another's negligence. The public policy of this state has been, in substance, to posit the risk of negligence upon the actor; in instances in which this policy has been abandoned, it has generally been to allow or require that the risk shift to another party better or equally able to bear it, not to shift the risk to the weak bargainer.

[2] In the light of the decisions, we think that the hospital-patient contract clearly falls within the category of agreements affecting the public interest. To meet that test, the agreement need only fulfill some of the characteristics above outlined; here, the relationship fulfills all of them. Thus the contract of exculpation involves an institution suitable for, and a subject of, public regulation [statutory citation omitted]. [Footnote omitted.] That the services of the hospital to those members of the public who are in special need of the particular skill of its staff and facilities constitute a practical and crucial necessity is hardly open to question.

The hospital, likewise, holds itself out as willing to perform its services for those members of the public who qualify for its research and training facilities. While it is true that the hospital is selective as to the patients it will accept, such selectivity does not negate its public aspect or the public interest in it. The hospital is selective only in the sense that it accepts from the public at large certain types of cases which qualify for the research and training in which it specializes. But the hospital does hold itself out to the public as an institution which performs such services for those members of the public who can qualify for them. [Footnote omitted.]

In insisting that the patient accept the provision of waiver in the contract, the hospital certainly exercises a decisive advantage in bargaining. The would-be patient is in no position to reject the proffered agreement, to bargain with the hospital, or in lieu of agreement to find another hospital. The admission room of a hospital contains no bargaining table where, as in a private business transaction, the parties can debate the terms of their contract. As a result, we cannot but conclude that the instant agreement manifested the characteristics of the so-called adhesion contract. Finally, when the patient signed the contract, he completely placed himself in the control of the hospital; he subjected himself to the risk of its carelessness.

In brief, the patient here sought the services which the hospital offered to a selective portion of the public; the patient, as the price of admission and as a result of his inferior bargaining position, accepted a clause in a contract of adhesion waiving the hospital's negligence; the patient thereby subjected himself to control of the hospital and the possible infliction of the negligence which he had thus been compelled to waive. The hospital, under such circumstances, occupied a status different than a mere private party; its contract with the patient affected the public interest. . . .

. . .

We must note, finally, that the integrated and specialized society of today, structured upon mutual dependency, cannot rigidly narrow the concept of the public interest. From the observance of simple standards of due care in the driving of a car to the performance of the high standards of hospital practice, the individual citizen must be completely dependent upon the responsibility of others. The fabric of this pattern is so closely woven that the snarling of a single thread affects the whole. We cannot lightly accept a sought immunity from careless failure to provide the hospital's service upon which many must depend. Even if the hospital's doors are open only to those in a specialized category, the hospital cannot claim isolated immunity in the interdependent community of our time. It, too, is part of the social fabric, and prearranged exculpation from its negligence must partly rend the pattern and necessarily affect the public interest.

The judgment is reversed.

GIBSON, C. J. and TRAYNOR, J., SCHAUER, J., McCOMB, J., PETERS, J., AND PEEK, J., concurred.

If you had written the allegedly offensive paragraph 6 "RELEASE," what defenses would you argue to the court? What was the writer trying to accomplish by inserting paragraph 6 into the contract? Is it good or bad? Why? From whose point of view? Should the draftsman of paragraph 6 have known better?

Would this clause be less offensive if its topic were binding arbitration for resolution of a personal injury claim due to malpractice of the hospital's physican employee? Would it make any difference if the arbitration clause was part of an employer-employee labor contract for medical care at the hospital in question? At any other hospital?

Which of the elements listed that make up an adhesion contract can be scrapped?

Admittedly difficult to define, where does the court find public policy? Where does the court get the wisdom to say what public policy is? Is the hospital a public utility? Should it be regulated as one? When does the individual physician become part of the medical industry? Is there such an entity? What is it comprised of? Is it homogeneous or heterogeneous in its composition? Does your being a member of that group influence your answer? If so, how?

Termination of Patient-Physician Contract

Although the patient can formally discharge his physician orally or in writing, practically all the patient has to do to terminate the patient-physician contract and/or relationship is either not return to the physician or choose another one. It is as simple as that.

For the physician, termination of the patient-physician relationship and/or contract is not so simple. Much of what he is expected to do depends upon the medical status of the patient. Generally, the physician is expected to give *timely notice* of his intention to *terminate* the contract so the patient will have the *opportunity* to obtain continuing medical care.

Notice means that the physician is obligated to inform his patient that the physician intends to terminate their patient-physician contract on a specific date in the future, and to advise the patient to get other medical care. This can be done in writing or orally. If the physician chooses to send the patient a letter, it is best to send it registered mail, return receipt requested. The return receipt is strong evidence that the patient received notice.

Timely means that the patient is given sufficient time to obtain other medical care. How long depends upon the surrounding circumstances. Generally, seven, ten, or fourteen days would seem adequate. Shorter or longer times may be appropriate in special circumstances. The court's criterion will be: under the circumstances, did the patient have a reasonable length of time to get other medical care? If the physician chooses to terminate the patient-physician contract orally, he is still obligated to give the timely notice of termination and the opportunity to get other medical care. A good way to terminate the contract orally is for the physician to inform the patient of the termination in front of two or three witnesses, then make and date a written memorandum outlining what he told the patient, have the witnesses sign the memorandum, and have the patient sign, too, if he will. A contemporaneously written memorandum of the oral termination is useful evidence for the physician should any dispute arise in the future over the termination of the patient-physician contract.

The *opportunity* requirement is met when the physician advises the patient to get other medical care and gives him enough time to do so. To avoid giving the impression of being abrupt or arbitrary, the physician ought to give his reasons for terminating the contract.

Breach of Contract and Duty

Should the physician fail to give the patient timely notice of his intention to terminate their contract, the physician is open to the charge of abandonment. Abandonment is the unilateral, unlawful termination of the patient-physician relationship. From the point of view of the patient-physician contract, it is a breach of *contract*.

From the point of view of negligence, it is a breach of the physician's duty to care for the patient diligently. Since the physician's duty is clearly spelled out and not in dispute, the issue in court is: what conduct of the defendant-physician constitutes breach of the duty? Each case must be analyzed on its own facts.

Premature discharge from the physician's care has been held to be abandonment. This is often associated with the physician's failure to give instructions on what to do or whom to call should untoward symptoms occur. Failure to supply any, adequate, or competent coverage on days off and vacation, as well as failure to give either the covering physician or the patient the requisite information about each other, have all been held to be abandonment.

Chapter
Five

Confidentiality

V

Ƨ Ƨ Ƨ Ƨ Ƨ Ƨ Ƨ Ƨ Ƨ Ƨ Ƨ Ƨ Ƨ

From the time people began to seek medical treatment, patients have recognized that, if their physician is to cure them or relieve their suffering, they must disclose sensitive information about themselves. When a patient does so, he fully expects his physician to respect and to preserve the confidence in which the sensitive information was given. Physicians have also recognized the necessity of keeping this sensitive information confidential; that is why most, if not all, codes of medical ethics counsel the physician not to discuss information gleaned from caring for the patient with others, except for the purpose of medical consultation.

Today, the three questions which arise concerning the confidentiality of the patient's medical history are: defamation (libel and slander), patient-physician privilege, and governmental intrusion.

Defamation: Libel and Slander

What remedy does the patient have if the physician should disclose information given to him, during diagnosis and treatment, in privacy and confidence? The law of defamation gives the patient a means of compensation for damage done to his reputation due to unauthorized or unprivileged disclosure of sensitive information to third persons by the physician. Alternatively, the law of defamation gives the physician an incentive to respect that confidence.

The gist of defamation is that the defamatory material which the defendant communicates to a third person or persons damages the plaintiff's reputation. The damage to the plaintiff's reputation may be the lowering of him in the esteem of others, holding him up to hatred or ridicule, or causing him to be shunned or ostracized. The reputation may be the plaintiff's personal, business, or professional reputation.

Slander is the oral communication of defamatory material to a third person or persons. Libel is communication of the defamatory material by written or printed materials. Whether printed, written, or oral, the technical term for communication of the defamatory material is *publication*.

Many pieces of information that the physician gathers in diagnosing and treating his patients have in the past been held to be defamatory *per se*. Defamatory per se, or defamatory on its face, means that the plaintiff does not have the burden of proving to the court that he suffered damage, as the plaintiff would ordinarily have to do, but only that the defendant published the defamatory material to a third person or persons who understood its defamatory message. For example, it has been held to be defamatory per se for a defendant to tell a third person that the plaintiff has a venereal disease or leprosy. Hence, the physician must be quite chary of what he says and with whom he discusses his patient's medical status.

In addition to pertinent, sensitive information about the patient, during the course of care the physician often learns sensitive, nonmedical information that is not pertinent, germane, or relevant to the care of that patient. Such information is best neither discussed further nor recorded in the chart.

In writing histories, especially about emergencies and on occasion other histories, the physician must be careful how he phrases what the patient tells him. What the patient says may defame a third person. If that statement is written down or repeated orally, that may be republication of the defamation. Republication is used here in the sense of communicating the defamatory material again. Such republication can and may subject the physician who recorded or repeated the history to a charge of libel or slander. This is especially so if the defamatory material accuses the third person of a crime, because accusing a person of a crime can be defamatory per se.

For the physician writing a medical history perhaps the best rule is to record only such information about his patient as is necessary to the diagnosis and treatment of that patient. Omit extraneous material.

Defenses

Because the law understands that people must at times communicate what amounts to defamatory information to others, it has carved out exceptions in the law of defamation, i.e., defenses or privileges, as they are called. Absolute privilege is a complete defense to a charge of defamation and arises in two situations: one, when the plantiff consents to the publication by the defendant (for example, the patient's authorization to release medical information to his health insurance carrier); two, publication of defamatory material in the course of judicial, executive, and legislative proceedings. Vis-a-vis the physician, judicial proceedings for the commitment of a patient to a mental institution are absolutely privileged. The rationale for each of these absolute privileges is self-evident.

Truth is, in most jurisdictions, a complete defense. However, in some jurisdictions by statute, truth is a complete defense to a charge of defamation *only if* the true statement was published for good motives or for justifiable ends. Otherwise, in these jurisdictions, truth is not a complete defense to defamation.

The law realizes that, on occasion, some defamatory material must be communicated to third persons for the benefit of society, the person possibly defamed, or the person publishing the libel or slander. Hence, the law has carved out a privilege or defense to fit this situation. It is called a qualified or conditional privilege; it is not absolute. To avail himself of this defense, the defendant must have exercised his good faith and judgment in communicating the defamatory material, as well as used reasonable care in what he said and to whom he said it and for what purpose he said it.

Even when the physician makes professional statements and renders medical opinions, the law of defamation treats him no differently from others. The physician can claim the qualified privilege of publishing otherwise actionable defamatory material (i) if the information is communicated in good faith and (ii) if both the physician and the third person to whom the information is given have a legal or moral obligation to, a social duty to, or interest in, the person about whom the information is communicated. Generally, a disinterested third person's overhearing defamatory material told to the physician by the patient does not defeat the conditional or qualified privilege.

Berry v. Moench, 8 Utah 2d 191, 331 P.2d 814, 73 A.L.R.2d 315 (1958), which follows, is an instructive case for physicians. First, it explores the dimensions of Dr. Moench's qualified or conditional privilege. Second, it raises the question of truth in the context of the veracity of his sources of information.

BERRY v. MOENCH

8 Utah 2d 191, 331 P.2d 814, 73 A.L.R.2d 315 (1958)

CROCKETT, Justice.

Robert J. Berry appeals from an adverse jury verdict

and judgment in a suit against Dr. Louis G. Moench for publishing in a letter allegedly false and derogatory information acquired in connection with treating Mr. Berry as a patient.

Significant portions of the letter are:

"Dear Dr. Hellewell:

"Since I do not have his authorization, the patient you mentioned in your last letter will remain nameless.

"He was treated here in 1949 as an emergency. Our diagnosis was Manic depressive depression in a psychopathic personality * * *

"He had one brother as a manic, and his father committed suicide * * *

"The patient was attempting to go through school on the G.I. bill * * * Instead of attending class he would spend most of the days and nights playing cards for money.

"Because of family circumstances, we treated him for a mere token charge (and I notice even that has never been paid).

"During his care here, he purchased a brand new Packard, without even money to buy gasoline.

"He was in constant trouble with the authorities during the war, * * *

"* * * did not do well in school, and never did really support his wife and children.

"Since he was here, we have repeated requests for his record indicating repeated trouble. * * *

"My suggestion to the infatuated girl would be to run as fast and as far as she possibly could in any direction away from him.

"Of course if he doesn't marry her, he will marry someone else and make life hell for that person. The usual story is repeated unsuccessful marriages and a trail of tragedy behind."

The above letter was written September 12, 1956, in response to one in which Dr. J. S. Hellewell of Evanston, Wyoming had requested information concerning Mr.

Berry, asking for "your impression of the man," for the stated purpose of passing it on to a Mr. and Mrs. Williams, parents of Mary Boothe who was then keeping company with Mr. Berry.

The information supplied by Dr. Moench had been obtained seven years earlier in connection with the psychiatric treatment of Mr. Berry. The latter had been having marital difficulties and at the request of his then wife, Ethella Berry, had gone to Dr. Moench. His condition was diagnosed; electric shock treatments recommended and four of them were given. Dr. Moench had not seen plaintiff since that time.

The letter was relayed by Dr. Hellewell to the Williamses and in turn to their daughter, Mary Boothe. Consequently the parents became violently opposed to the marriage. They have since disowned their daughter because she went ahead and married the plaintiff and they are now husband and wife.

In justification of writing the letter, Dr. Moench relied on these defenses: That the statements were true; that he had a reasonable basis for believing them to be true; that he made them under conditional privilege; and that they were not defamatory.

At the pre-trial the court ruled as a matter of law that the doctor had a conditional privilege to make the statements. At the trial the jury was so instructed; and that any finding of malice must be shown by evidence independent of the letter; and also that if the statements were true, or if the doctor had probable cause to believe the statements to be true, that would constitute a defense. These rulings are here assigned as error.

It is recognized that ordinarily the truth is a defense to an action for libel or slander. However, in the instant case there is the special circumstance to reckon with, that a doctor-patient relationship existed between the parties in connection with which Dr. Moench acquired the information upon which he based the letter. That relationship is among those with respect to which it is the policy of the law to encourage confidence. This policy is expressed in Sec. 78-24-8, U.C.A. 1953 which provides, inter alia, that a physician cannot be examined as to any information acquired in attending his patient.[1] It is grounded upon the advantage to all concerned in encouraging the full disclosure of all facts which may have a bearing upon diagnosis and treatment of the patient. If the doctor could with impunity publish anything that is true, the patient would be without protection from disclosure of intimacies which might be both embarrassing and harmful to him. This would make him reluctant to tell some things even though they might be important in the treatment of his ills. For this reason it is obligatory upon the doctor not to reveal information obtained in confidence in connection with the diagnosis or treatment of his patient. It is our opinion that if the doctor violates that confidence and publishes derogatory matter concerning his patient, an action would lie for any injury suffered. That, of course, presupposes the absence of any privilege, as hereinafter discussed. Compare the obiter dicta statement of the Supreme Court of Washington, "* * * for so palpable a wrong, the law provides a remedy," which statement was similarly quoted with approval by the Nebraska Supreme Court in Simonsen v. Swenson [citation omitted]. That Dr. Moench himself was aware of his duty not to reveal the secrets of his patient without the latter's consent is shown in the letter, "Since I do not have his authorization, the patient * * * will remain nameless. * * *"

[1] We do not doubt the correctness of defendant's contention that the responsibility of the doctor to keep confidence may be outweighed by a higher duty to give out information, even though defamatory, if there is a sufficiently important interest to protect. In such event there arises a conditional privilege to make a disclosure reasonably necessary to protect such interest.

The usual situation giving rise to the privilege is where the interest being protected is that of the publisher . . . . Dr. Moench had no interest which was being protected by giving out this information.

---

[1]Sec. 78–24–8, U.C.A. 1953: Privileged Communications: also prohibits testimony re communications between: husband-wife; attorney-client; priest-confessor; physician-patient.

It should be kept in mind that this is not a situation where a patient had gone to a second doctor for treatment and the latter requested information from the first doctor to assist him in the diagnosis. Conceding that professional custom and comity require that this be permitted in a proper case for the help and protection of both doctors and patients, this is not such a case. Dr. Hellewell had never seen Mr. Berry and had no concern with him as a patient.

[2] We recognize that such a privilege may also extend to the protection of the interests of third persons under proper circumstances. Where life, safety, well-being or other important interest is in jeopardy, one having information which could protect against the hazard, may have a conditional privilege to reveal information for such purpose, even though it be defamatory and may prove to be false.[2] But the privilege is not something which arises automatically and becomes absolute merely because there is an interest to protect. It has its origin in, and it is governed by, the rule of good sense and customary conduct of people motivated by good will and proper consideration for others. This includes due consideration for the subject being informed about as well as the recipient being protected. The policy of the law concerning this matter is framed in the light of the hazard that defamation can so easily undermine or destroy a most precious possession: a good name and reputation. In ancient writ it is said "A good name is rather to be chosen than great riches."[3] Recognizing that a good name is so hard to acquire and to preserve, yet so vulnerable to being tarnished, the law imposes upon one publishing derogatory information, even for laudatory purposes, the responsibility of exercising due care in what he does and in knowing whereof he speaks.

[3] One purveying such information about one person to protect another is obligated to consider the likelihood and the extent of benefit to the recipient, if the matter is true, as compared with the likelihood of injury and the ex-

---

[2]A.L.I. Restatement of Torts, Sec. 595, et seq.
[3]Proverbs 22.1.

tent thereof to the subject, if it prove false, or improper to reveal. Whether the privilege exists, depends upon generally accepted standards of decent conduct. Applying that standard, it exists if the recipient has the type of interest in the matter, and the publisher stands in such a relation to him, that it would reasonably be considered the duty of the publisher to give the information.[4] If the facts upon which the privilege would rest are not in dispute, whether the privilege exists is a question for the court to determine. If they are in dispute the jury must determine the facts and upon them the court determines the question of privilege.[5]

[4] We are not disposed to disagree with the trial court's ruling that the circumstances here came within the framework of conditional privilege: that is, that Mary Boothe's concern for her well-being and happiness was a sufficient interest to protect, and that it was within the generally accepted standards of decent conduct for the doctor to reveal the information which might have an important bearing thereon. We believe, however, that that is as far as the trial court could go. In submitting the case to the jury on the basis of privilege it was necessary to instruct it as to the limitations upon the manner in which the privilege should be exercised.

[5] We are aware that it is frequently stated that where the situation is privileged there is no liability in the absence of actual malice [citation omitted]. However, an examination of the authorities reveals that quite generally, when the matter is actually in issue, they are in accord upon a principle which we consider sound and salutary: that the privilege to pass on derogatory information, which proves false, must have been exercised with at least reasonable discretion, or the publisher will be held responsible therefor. This is well summarized in the Restatement of Torts:

"Even though the occasion is so privileged, a par-

---

[4]See footnote 2 supra Sec. 595.
[5]Ibid, Sec. 619.

ticular person cannot avail himself of the privilege
arising therefrom if he abuses the occasion * * * The
occasion may be abused by the publisher's lack of belief or reasonable grounds for belief in the truth of the
defamatory matter * * *; by the publication of the
defamatory matter for some improper purpose * * *;
by excessive publication * * *; or by the publication
of defamatory matter not reasonably believed to be
necessary to accomplish the purpose.* * *"[6]

[6] It is significant that the privilege we are here
concerned with is referred to as a "conditional" or
"qualified" privilege. The reason for the limiting adjectives
is that it must be exercised with certain cautions: (a) it must
be done in good faith and reasonable care must be
exercised as to its truth, (b) likewise, the information must
be reported fairly, (c) only such information should be
conveyed, and (d) only to such persons as are necessary to
the purpose. We comment upon them as applicable to the
instant case.

[7] (a) It seems hardly necessary to state that one cannot
pass on derogatory information indifferent to its truth, or
the consequences thereof, but failure to exercise reasonable
care and diligence to ascertain the truth destroys the
privilege.[7] Dr. Moench was uncertain as to what
information came from what sources: the referring doctor
(Dr. Miller), the plaintiff, or plaintiff's then wife, Ethella
Berry, or her sister. Experience teaches that an unhappy
wife of a blighted marriage is not usually the most impartial source of information as to the conduct and character of a disappointing husband; less so a sister-in-law.
Nevertheless, Dr. Moench admitted relying on their statements.

As might be expected, plaintiff sharply disagrees as to

---

[6]A.L.I. Restatement of Torts, Sec. 595. . . .

[7]As was stated by the Pennsylvania Court [citation omitted]:
"Want of reasonable care and diligence to ascertain the truth,
***will destroy the privilege." (Citing cases.)

facts about him as assumed and reported by Dr. Moench. Illustrative are these:

Dr. Moench: that the plaintiff did not do well in school;

Plaintiff: grade school: I was in the top of my class every year; high school: finished in the top 1% of my class, editor-in-chief of the school paper, on student council and participated in other activities; college: in three years grades were above average, admitted flunking two courses.

Dr. Moench: that he was in constant trouble with the authorities * * *

Plaintiff: this simmered down to about three incidents of minor importance.

Dr. Moench: purchased a new Packard without even money to buy gasoline;

Plaintiff: that he had $200 in the bank and received $4,000 inheritance.

Dr. Moench: that he had not paid his bill.

Plaintiff: that of the charge of $50, all but $5 had long since been paid.

As to the latter item, the doctor relied on a red tab on the card, indicating an unpaid bill. He admitted that checking his record would have revealed the fact that all but $5 had been paid.

[8] (b) Closely related to the duty to use reasonable diligence as to truth is the requirement that the publisher communicate the information fairly. He is not warranted in reporting as undoubted facts information which may have been derived from sources which render its verity questionable. If it is from mere hearsay or there are other circumstances which would render it open to suspicion of unsoundness, fairness requires him to report such circumstances along with the information.[8] This is especially important as to a doctor. His professional status and his duty to keep the confidence of his patient tend to endow information he gives with more than ordinary credibility. In regard to this requirement, plaintiff makes these points: that the doctor was advising about his present condition, based upon skimpy, unverified information obtained seven

---

[8]A.L.I. Restatement of Torts, Sec. 602, comment a.

years earlier, which he assumed to be true and stated as facts, without stating the source; that even if plaintiff had been mentally ill at the prior time, it was wrong to assume that he was still so afflicted; and also for the doctor to fail to make any allowance for the possibility of his getting well, or even that his own treatments had any beneficial effect; particularly so when the doctor on cross examination stated that he had treated about 800 patients with this ailment with such success that most of them were getting along quite well and making a success of their marriages.

[9] (c) Another aspect of the situation to be considered is the requirement, even under a privileged situation, that only such information should be given as is necessary for the purpose for which the privilege exists.[9] E.g., if the fact that the bill had not been paid had any bearing on the situation, which may be open to question, reasonable effort to supply accurate information should be made. The same observation is pertinent to other items set forth above.

[10] (d) There is further question, admittedly more tenuous than the others, as to whether the publication was to more persons than reasonably necessary to afford the protection for which the privilege existed.[10] Neither Mary Boothe nor Mr. Berry were patients of Dr. Moench or Dr. Hellewell, nor had any personal relationship of any character with them. Dr. Hellewell was not acting as a physician to either of them, nor to the Williamses. His only objective was in doing what he regarded as a favor to the Williamses who had been his patients. He can properly be regarded only as an intermediary, who was intended to pass the information on through other intermediaries, the Williamses, to the person directly concerned. The likelihood of the parents being greatly concerned and disposed to talk to others about the matter may be taken into account. Conceding that Mary Boothe had such an interest that Dr. Moench properly thought she should be given the information, it seems to us that reasonable minds might entertain the thought that a more direct method of getting the information to her should have been employed than to

---

[9]Ibid, Sec. 595, comment a. and Sec. 605.
[10]Ibid, Sec. 604.

relay it through others, even though they had made the inquiry in her interest.

[11] It may well be that Dr. Moench did that which was discreet and proper with respect to the principles discussed under (a), (b), (c) and (d) above. We do not presume to say. It appears to us that the evidence provides a basis upon which reasonable minds might differ as to whether he did so in connection with the passing on of information of the character in question. Thus such issues should have been submitted to the jury. Inasmuch as the manner in which the case was submitted did not permit the jury to pass on these issues it is necessary for us to remand the cause for a new trial. In doing so it is incumbent upon us to comment on certain matters that will be pertinent on the retrial [citation omitted].

[12, 13] Libel may be defined as a false and unprivileged publication in writing which assails the honesty, integrity or virtue of another and thereby exposes him to hatred, contempt, or ridicule, or tends to injure him in his occupation [citation omitted]. The letter can be regarded as doing so.

[14, 15] In the law of defamation there is an important difference between the term "malice" when used to denote actual malice, or as it is sometimes called, "malice in fact," as contrasted with implied malice or "malice in law." Actual malice or malice in fact may be found only when it appears that the actor was motivated by spite, hatred or ill will against the subject and it must exist before punitive damages can be awarded. There is a lack of proof of the latter type of malice in this case. Malice in law, which is a necessary prerequisite to recovery for libel, may be implied from the intentional doing of the wrongful act of uttering defamatory matter which is false, or without legal justification [citation omitted]. Whether such malice existed in the utterance is to be determined from all of the facts and circumstances shown by the evidence, including the contents of the letter [citation omitted].

Remanded for a new trial. Costs to appellant.

WADE and WORTHEN, JJ., concur.

McDONOUGH, C. J., and HENRIOD, J., concur in the result.

[Footnotes renumbered.]

Patient-Physician Privilege

Can a patient prevent his physician in court, who is under oath, from answering questions about sensitive information that was revealed in the consulting chamber or sickroom? At English Common Law, the patient did not have this privilege; the physician had to answer these questions. Some state legislatures, however, considered this rule of law detrimental to the patient-physician therapeutic relationship. As a result, these states enacted statutes that permit the *patient* to enforce the confidentiality of information given to the physician in the course of diagnosis and treatment. In contravention to the common law rule, these laws establish a patient-physician privilege, which is personal to the patient. Some states define the privilege to cover information given to all physicians; others only to psychiatrists.

Here is how the privilege works: if the patient's physician is on the witness stand under oath and is asked a question about information that the physician received from the patient as part of diagnosis and treatment, the patient can prevent the physician from answering that and similar questions. The patient's attorney objects to the question on the basis of the patient-physician privilege; the judge sustains the objection and directs the physician not to answer the question.

The patient, through his attorney, must claim the privilege. On the other hand, the physician cannot refuse to answer the question on the basis of the patient-physician privilege (the privilege is personal to the patient).

Obviously, if the patient puts his health at issue in a lawsuit, such as a personal injury suit or a malpractice suit, then the patient is said to have waived the privilege. For the patient to exercise the privilege in such cases would be palpably unfair to the defendant.

Government Computers

With the increasing governmental surveillance of medical practice and the need for government to collect medical statistics, how can the patient prevent the dissemination of sensitive information about himself to nonprofessionals for nonmedical purposes? This question raises a whole host of subsidiary questions, such as: what information shall go into the government's computers? Who shall, legally or otherwise, gain access to that computer information? How can the confidentiality of computer stored medical information be established and maintained?

The original question, rephrased in social, political, or economic terms, becomes: whose right is paramount, the patient's legitimate expectation of the confidentiality of his medical information, or the government's need to know and manipulate medical information? It can be expected that random legislative solutions will be put forth to answer some of the subsidiary questions as they arise. The determination of whose right or rights are paramount will have to wait until the situation can be viewed from the perspective of time.

Chapter
Six

Medical Records as an Introduction to the Rules of Evidence

VI

The Rules of Evidence or the Law of Evidence is part of a larger body of law that governs *how* a trial is conducted. "How" implies procedure or process; this larger body of law is termed Procedural Law. A person can sue or be sued in contract for breach of contract or in tort for negligence, but there is no such thing as suing or being sued in evidence. The basic concept of the rules of evidence is the orderly presentation of the appropriate facts needed, traditionally used, or required to settle an issue in dispute at trial.

Except for abstract and esoteric discussions, most discussions of the rules of evidence must be carried on within the context of torts, crimes, or contracts: what facts or physical evidence (the murder weapon) the attorney is trying to introduce into evidence, and what the attorney is trying to prove with the evidence offered.

Whether oral testimony or physical evidence, the law demands that the evidence be not only truthful but also the best available evidence. If the terms of a contract are in dispute, the court demands the original document signed by the parties. If this is unavailable, the court will, by force of circumstances, have to accept that which is next best, perhaps a conformed copy. Least acceptable, because of all its vagaries, is the oral testimony of the parties as to the contents of the unavailable written contract.

The courts value as evidence reliable data that are accurately recorded at the time of the event and also consider it an excellent aid to refresh a witness's memory about his observations and opinions of the event. In addition to demanding truthful, accurate, and the best available evidence, the courts further demand that the evidence come from a competent source and be both relevant and material to the dispute at hand. Competent means that the person testifying must convince the judge that he knows enough about the issue in dispute to be heard.

There are many true facts available that do not lead to the

resolution of a dispute; these are not received in evidence. Those facts that do lead to a dispute's resolution are said to be relevant and material to the issue at hand and are therefore accepted into evidence for consideration by the jury.

We will now look at the problems posed by attempting to introduce the patient's clinical record (chart) into evidence in a personal injury case — malpractice or auto accident.

From the medical point of view, the patient's clinical record helps the physician care for his patient. In it are recorded the patient's symptoms, signs, physical examinations, laboratory data, and other reports, as well as the attending physicians' and consultants' diagnoses, differential diagnoses, treatment plans, and the reasons therefor. Traditionally, the data contained in the patient's clinical chart are recorded as nearly contemporaneously as possible with the event, then signed and dated. Usually the patient's office and hospital clinical records are kept for future use.

From the legal point of view, the patient's clinical record is a pivotal source of information which can convince the patient's attorney that the patient either *may* have or does *not* have a cause of action against the physician or other person(s). If the patient's attorney feels that his client may have a cause of action, then how much of the patient's clinical record can the attorney introduce at trial for the jury's consideration?

The party offering the patient's clinical record into evidence (for the court's consideration) must first connect it to the patient; that is to say, prove it is what it purports to be. To do this, the hospital record librarian convinces the court that he has been custodian of the patient's chart, and that the name, number, and other data on the clinical record refer to the patient who is now a party to this lawsuit. In short, the patient's clinical record must be authenticated.

IF the writer of each note in the patient's clinical record were to give his material orally in court, the writer of the note would be under oath (an insurance of truth), subject to cross-examination (an insurance of truth), and the jury would have the opportunity to judge his credibility (an insurance of truth). However, none of these insurances of truth are available to the court when only the patient's clinical record as such is offered into evidence.

Now, if a note in the patient's clinical record is offered in evidence to show the truth of what the writer wrote, and if the writer is not in court, that note is "hearsay" and subject to exclusion or is inadmissible into evidence. That is to say, the note is offered for the truth of the statement without the safeguards of its truth—the oath, cross-examination, and the jury's opportunity to assess the writer's credibility.

A digression here to explore hearsay evidence by examining this witness's statement: "Joe said, 'The red and green checked VW hit the parked car.' "

Whether that statement is hearsay or not depends upon the purpose for which it is offered into evidence. If it is offered to show that "Joe" was awake, alert, and observant enough to make the statement, it can be accepted into evidence. The truthfulness of the witness is at stake— not the content of "Joe's" utterance. If it is offered to show that "Joe" was not mute but able to speak at that time, it can be accepted into evidence. If it is offered to show that the witness and "Joe" did have a conversation, it can be accepted into evidence.

But if the statement is offered for the truth of the statement's contents, that the red and green checked VW did in fact hit the parked car, AND if "Joe" is not in court (not available to take the oath nor subject to cross-examination nor present for the jury to see and hear) it is hearsay and excluded from evidence. Alternatively, it is hearsay because the jury has no way of verifying the statement's truth or falsity.

Because much of the business in everyday life is transacted on hearsay, the courts have had to carve out numerous exceptions to the hearsay rule. All the exceptions have in common some item or items that both insure the truth of the statement and let the court dispense with the oath, cross-examination, and the jury's viewing of the witness while he testifies.

The patient's clinical record comes under the Hearsay Rule's Business Record exception. Concisely, this exception says that contemporaneously recorded data that are recorded "in the usual course of business" for business purposes are presumed (but not conclusively presumed) accurate and truthful. This presumption arises because it would not be in the business's best interest to keep inaccurate or untruthful records, and because, in general, people are truthful. The court accepts five items (written data, recorded contemporaneously with the event, in the usual course of business, for business purposes, and lack of incentive to lie) in lieu of the oath, cross-examination, and viewing of the witness by the jury.

Because the business record is not conclusively presumed to be truthful, the opposing party can challenge the statement and show it is biased, prejudiced, or untrue. Nevertheless, it has been admitted into evidence despite its being hearsay; now, its truthfulness and weight are for the jury to determine.

The patient's clinical record is kept in the usual course of caring for the patient (the physician's business). It is kept for the benefit of the patient's care and very little would be gained by keeping an inaccurate or untrue record. These items are sufficient safeguards of the truth for the courts to dispense with the oath, cross-examination, and the jury's observation of the witness. Therefore, the patient's clinical record is accepted into evidence for the truth of the statements contained therein.

However, there is one caveat. Should the record be kept in contemplation of a lawsuit, it is supect as a self-serving document of the maker or the patient.

In summary, although parts or all of the patient's clinical record may be hearsay and subject to exclusion, its contents are admissible under the Business Records exception to the Hearsay Rule.

Extraneous material in the patient's clinical record is also subject to exclusion. For example, if, in the admitting statement, the physician recorded, "That drunken bum ran a stop sign at 75 miles an hour and hit me," most of the statement would be excluded because it is not in the usual course of the physician's business to record such statements; and, except for the fact that the patient said he was involved in a motor vehicle accident, the statement is irrelevant to the physician's care of the patient. Furthermore, it may be the patient's self-serving statement. For these reasons, most of it is excluded from evidence.

A further caveat: such a statement may be libellous because it accuses the person referred to of committing three crimes — drunken driving, running a stop sign, and speeding. Should the physician repeat the statement orally or write it in the record, the physician exposes himself to a charge of, and the possibility of liability for, republishing the slanderous statement.

Expert Testimony

The jury is conclusively presumed to be endowed with the ordinary and common knowledge of the community. However, some fields of knowledge, medicine among them, are not considered to be within the jury's fund of ordinary and common knowledge. For this reason, when medical issues arise at trial, persons with training, experience, and expertise in the field are required. They are termed expert witnesses.

One side or the other usually foresees an issue that requires expert testimony and offers such testimony. If the judge decides that expert testimony is needed to resolve an issue at trial, he listens to the proffered expert's qualifications and then decides whether or not the proffered expert will be heard as an expert witness.

Experts are needed in two situations, which frequently overlap. One, the expert has information or facts the jury needs; he gives the facts to the jury; it draws its conclusions. Two, the jury has the appropriate facts before it but is unable to draw inferences and conclusions from these facts because of lack of expertise; the jury then hears the expert draw his conclusions from the facts. To get the facts before the expert, the hypothetical question is used.

The opposing party can challenge the expert on the basis of his training, experience, expertise, bias, prejudice, or because he does not practice in a community of comparable size or some other factor similar to that of the opposing party. The latter is called the Locality Rule. It is now under attack and attrition in those states where it is still extant.

Chapter
Seven

Agency

VII

The term "agency" covers that body of law relating to one person working for another's benefit. This material is brought together here to show how a legal relationship between two persons can influence relationships to third persons.

The roots of this ancient body of law are in the status of master and servant. Although people were born to the status of either master or servant, there were laws regulating their respective rights and duties to one another.

With the advent of widespread trade, it became necessary for one person to have the power to make binding contracts for the benefit of another. Usually there was a contract between principal and agent. The touchstone of whether an agent can bind his principal to a contract with third parties is: did the principal clothe the agent with sufficient indicia of authority so as to lead a third party into believing an agency relationship existed? An important corollary to this is that "the agent cannot establish his own agency." Only the principal can. The law of principal and agency developed from the law of master-servant.

The current employer-employee relationship is a blend of master-servant and principal-agent law. Today, a contract of employment replaces status; whether or not the employee can bind his employer to a contract depends upon the terms and setting of employment. Because the law of master-servant is the forerunner of employer-employee law, these terms are often used interchangeably when the courts discuss, or try to decide, what relationship exists between two persons so that a legal determination of their respective rights and duties can be made.

If there is no written contract to guide the court, it must look to the dealings between the individuals to determine just what relationship existed between them in fact.

Independent Contractor

Perhaps the best starting point is when one person engages another to perform a service or produce an item on a one-time basis. In this situation, the person doing the work is expected to produce the item or provide the service, often using the specifications of the person engaging him, but working independently (without the engaging person's supervision or control). The person doing the work is said to be an independent contractor. What this means is that the law of contract applies to their dealings; and, if the independent contractor negligently injures a third person, the engaging party is not liable nor are they jointly liable. The party causing the injury is liable. One caveat: if the engaging party negligently selects or puts the engaged party who is known to be negligent in a situation where others are likely to be injured, the engaging party is liable on a negligence theory.

In the medical context, is the hospital-based pathologist an employee of the hospital or an independent contractor? Before answering this question, one must ask who are the disputing parties? Is the dispute between the hospital and the pathologist? The patient and the pathologist? The patient and the hospital? Phrased differently, is it a matter of contract or tort, i.e., malpractice or a nonprofessionally caused injury? Alternatively, into whose pocket does the court's hand reach to pay a successful plaintiff?

Master-Servant

The touchstone of the master is that he has the right of control over the servant. So far as the court is concerned, it is the master's right of control over the servant's actions that is important, not whether he exercised that control. To establish whether the putative master had the right of control, the court looks to whether or not the putative master can hire, fire, determine the salary, pay it, and set working conditions and hours. If he does some or all of these things, then the relationship between the parties is likely to be held one of master and servant (employer-employee).

The following case, *Hodges v. Doctors Hospital*, 141 Ga. App. 649, 234 S.E.2d 116 (1977), shows how the hospital used the defense of independent contractor to counter the plaintiff's allegations of an employer-employee relationship.

HODGES v. DOCTORS HOSPITAL
141 Ga. App. 649, 234 S.E.2d 116 (1977)

QUILLIAN, Presiding Judge.

The plaintiffs, husband and children of the deceased, sought recovery against the defendant hospital for negligent treatment resulting in the decedent's death. The case was tried and at the close of plaintiff's evidence a verdict was directed for the defendant. Appeal was taken from the judgment entered on the verdict. *Held:*

• • •

2. The sole question raised by appellant is whether the evidence demanded a finding in favor of the defendant hospital. This necessarily involves a determination of whether the doctor who treated the deceased and whose alleged negligence caused the wrongful death was an employee of the hospital or was an independent contractor.

The appellee urges the applicability of the ruling found in *Clary v. Hospital Auth.*, 106 Ga.App. 134 (1) (126 SE2d 470) and subsequently followed in *Pogue v. Hospital Auth.*, 120 Ga.App. 230 (170 SE2d 53): "Ordinarily, a physician or surgeon on the staff of a hospital is not an employee of such hospital, and in the absence of allegations that the hospital was negligent in the selection of an unskillful physician or surgeon or that the hospital undertook to direct him in the way and manner of treating the patient, the hospital is not liable for the mere negligent performance of professional services by a physician or surgeon on its staff."

. . . *Clary* stands only for the principle that a physician on the staff of a hospital is not automatically an employee of the hospital and where a physician is an independent contractor the hospital is not liable for his negligent performance of professional services unless it negligently selected him or undertook to direct him in the manner and method of treating the patient.

In ascertaining what relation exists, the requirements are neither complex nor uncertain but their application is extremely difficult. The true test of whether the relationship is one of employer-employee or employer-independent contractor is whether the employer, under the contract either oral or written, assumes the right to control the time, manner and method of executing the work, as distinguished from the right merely to require certain definite results in conformity to the contract. [Citations omitted.]

Judge (now Justice) Jordan pointed out the inherent problems involved in *Travelers Ins. Co. v. Moates*, 102 Ga.App. 778, 781 (117 SE2d 924): "Where the question of control is not discussed at the time the service is engaged, and where it never arises during performance, it is often exceedingly difficult to determine whether the employer had, or intended to reserve, such right. However, it has been held in a number of decisions that where one is employed generally to perform certain services for another, and there is no specific contract to do a certain piece of work according to specifications for a stipulated sum, it is inferable that the employer has retained the right to control the manner, method and means of the performance of the contract, and that the employee is not an independent contractor." [Citations omitted.]

It should be emphasized that the important consideration is not whether the employer exercised control over the time and manner of executing the work but whether the employer retained the right to do so. [Citation omitted.]

· · ·

Vicarious Liability

In addition to being held liable for his own malpractice, the physician can be held liable for the negligence of others. During his practice, the physician often directs or controls the activities of a person or persons other than his patients. For example, he directs or has control over what his office nurse, secretary, and office assistant do while they are working for him. Although medical students, interns, residents, and hospital nurses do not work for him in the usual sense, the physician may have control over or responsibility for their actions. Within the period the physician has the right to control their actions, he can be held liable for their negligence.

The doctrine of vicarious liability developed from the master-servant status. When this doctrine developed, a servant who negligently injured a person within the scope of his employment (while furthering the master's business) was unlikely to have sufficient funds to pay the injured plaintiff money damages. This left an innocently injured plaintiff to bear the burden of his injury. An unrecompensed, innocently injured plaintiff was considered raw justice. Besides, the injured plaintiff and his family might become a burden on family, friends, neighbors, and the local government's treasury. Since the master (employer) benefitted from his servant's efforts, it was felt, as between the innocently injured plaintiff and the master, that the latter should bear the burden of the plaintiff's injury, when the impecunious servant couldn't pay.

The doctrine of vicarious liability means that the one with the right of control pays money damages to the successful plaintiff. The tacit assumption is that the master has a deeper pocket than the servant. Translated into Latin, this becomes *respondeat superior*—let the master respond (in money damages).

Once the person with the right of control has paid the damages, he steps into the shoes of the plaintiff; in other words, he succeeds to all the rights of the plaintiff to sue the servant for the damages that the master paid. Obviously, if the injured plaintiff couldn't collect from the impecunious negligent servant, how does the court expect the one who had control to collect? In effect, the plaintiff is paid out of the deep pocket. As might be expected, those who have the responsibility for others today rarely sue them to recover the money they've paid out; they insure against such events.

To summarize: the servant who negligently caused the injury within the scope of his duties is primarily liable; the master is said to be secondarily liable or vicariously liable. Under this doctrine, the master himself is not negligent, but is financially responsible.

Borrowed Servant

In the operating suite, there is no doubt that the hospital employs the scrub nurse. During an operation, suppose the scrub nurse negligently injures the patient. Who pays? The nurse is likely to be impecunious. The hospital is likely to defend on the basis that, while the scrub nurse is at the operating table, the hospital does not have control over her actions, either theoretically or practically. The surgeon has control over what she does. The hospital's position is that they have lent the services of the scrub nurse to the surgeon for the operation. Viewed alternatively, the scrub nurse is a borrowed servant. As might be expected, the borrowing master is liable, because he has the right of control.

Parenthetically, at one time the courts tried to categorize the task that the scrub nurse negligently performed as either administrative or professional. If the negligently performed task was administrative, the hospital was held liable. If it was professional, the operating surgeon was held liable. Is the final sponge count before the surgeon closes the abdomen a professional or administrative task? Attempts to categorize the tasks led to some tortured rationalizations before the courts gave up this line of analysis.

Principal-Agent

The solo medical practitioner is a small businessman. He delivers services and charges for them; he pays overhead, rent, and taxes; and, if he has a secretary-receptionist and office nurse, he pays their salaries, insurance plans, and social security. The more physicians who practice together, the larger their business. Society through the exercise of its laws has no trouble in viewing and holding the nonprofessional side of medical practice to the same rules and standards as any other business.

As a proprietor of a small business, the physician can be made a party to a contract which he may not be aware of and to which he would rather not be a party. A simple example is: the physician's office nurse telephones a supplier, identifies herself, and orders 500 plastic disposable gloves. Supplier delivers them and sends a bill. Even though the physician never heard of supplier, he has to pay. Office nurses can reasonably be expected to keep the physician in examining gloves. The gloves are to be used for the physician's benefit in running his business. Obviously, the office nurse isn't going to pay for them out of her own pocket, even though she ordered them. It is eminently reasonable that she be able to make her employer, the physician, a party to a contract for his benefit. Her purchase was within the scope of her apparent authority as office nurse.

It goes without saying that it is outside of the office nurse's apparent authority to bind the physician to a contract for a shiny, new, fire engine red Cadillac. Purchase of expensive office furniture or sophisticated medical equipment, or contracting for major remodeling jobs are examples of contracts that are beyond the scope of the office nurse's employment.

The physician's neglect of "minor details" may also bind him to unwanted contracts. Suppose the physician handed a mockup of a billhead to his secretary with a notation, "Get 1,000." He told her to get them for $.01 apiece or less. Secretary ordered a thousand at $.025 apiece. The billheads were what the physician wanted, but not at that price. He had to pay. Why?

From the printer's point of view, the physician had given secretary a specimen of what he wanted with a notation that reasonably meant, purchase one thousand. To the printer, the physician had clothed the secretary with sufficient indicia of authority to establish a principal-agent relationship. What the printer didn't know, and didn't have reason to know, was that she had special instructions as to price. Although the secretary exceeded her authority, the printer had no reason to check with the physician about special instructions. The physician had to pay for the billheads as billed.

The physician must be extremely careful in clothing his agents with authority, especially those who handle money. One Friday, the day the physician had selected for his office manager to deposit all the checks he received that week, the physician needed $250 in cash for a weekend trip. He told his office manager to deposit the checks as usual but to get $250 in cash for him. When the teller spotted the $250 withdrawal, he checked with a vice president, who called the physician to see if this withdrawal was proper. Physician assured the vice president that it was all right to give the office manager cash whenever deposits were made.

At the end of the year, the physician's accountant found that the office manager had continued to pick up $250 more or less regularly for her own use.

The bank, through its employees, did all it could. When they saw the office manager (agent) withdrawing the funds, they checked with the physician (principal), who assured them it was proper for the bank to deliver cash to his office manager whenever she made her Friday deposits. Physician had clothed his office manager with authority that could be abused. As principal, physician had to bear the loss, or try to recover it from his office manager — or the bonding company, if the physician had had his employees who handle money bonded against just such thefts.

Chapter
Eight

The Hospital and
the Physician

VIII

The physician should read this chapter in the light of "as others see us." Currently, society perceives the physician not so much as independently caring for the acutely ill patient but as part of an integrated institution, the "medical industry," whose focal point is the hospital. The hospital is perceived as capable of providing preventive, diagnostic, and consultive, as well as acute and chronic treatment facilities. The integration of the physician into the hospital occurs naturally because, today, without access to the modern hospital for his patients, the physician is severely hamstrung in caring for them.

Because society is changing its focus from individual physician's care of the ill patient to the hospital, society is looking increasingly to the hospital for redress of medically related injuries. Following this perception, the courts are placing greater responsibility on the hospital for both the individual patient's care and for the overall level of medical practice within that institution. Together with the hospital's increased responsibility comes its right and power to require the medical staff to monitor their medical performance. On the other hand, although the hospital as a corporate entity has always had the responsibility and the accompanying right to monitor—police if you will—medical practice within it, until now it has neither assumed that responsibility nor exercised that right. Furthermore, because the hospital is the focus of much medical care, the federal government has found it convenient to use hospitals and their organized medical staffs as its base of operations for controlling part of the cost of health care. For these reasons, physicians ought to understand how hospitals are organized and managed and also what their responsibilities are to their patients.

The Hospital as the Physician's Workshop

Hospitals are enterprises whose function is to care for the sick. They fulfill the purpose of caring for patients by offering the physician both a place for, and the facilities for, diagnosing and treating his patients. Note: the hospital's purpose is to "care for," not to treat patients. The law is clear: a corporation cannot practice medicine!

The vast majority of hospitals are nonprofit enterprises. This evolved because hospitals were originally established and run by religious orders and/or were eleemosynary (alms supported) institutions. In the past, the courts held that hospitals had charitable immunity from tort liability. This meant that, if in the course of employment a hospital employee negligently injured someone, the hospital as employer (master) was immune from paying money damages to the injured plaintiff. The theory here was that the hospital was run on alms freely given to care for the sick, and not to pay money judgments. In addition, paying money judgments might bankrupt the hospital, whose services the community needed. With time, the financial management of the hospital changed from that of alms supported to that of a business operation. As a result, most states have abandoned the doctrine of charitable immunity for hospitals and now treat them as any other employer whose employee has negligently injured someone.

The Hospital as a Corporation

Any enterprise devoted to the care of the sick will of necessity be a complex operation financially and professionally. With the advent of the corporation, it was only natural that hospitals would formalize their organization and take up corporate status.

A corporation is an entity set up with legislative permission to accomplish some specific task or tasks as set out in the corporate charter. Prior to corporations, the voluntary associations of individuals that ran an enterprise were partnerships. However, under partnership law, each partner is financially liable not only for his own personal debts, but also for the personal debts of his individual partners and for the debts of the partnership, the enterprise. This means that a large enterprise having many partners forces each partner to assume a potentially ruinous burden of personal debt.

Under corporate law, the corporation alone is responsible for its debts. By giving corporate status to the enterprise, each individual organizer shields his personal assets not only from the corporation's creditors but also from the other organizers' creditors. In other words, for creditors to satisfy their claims against the corporation, they are limited to looking to the corporation's assets. Hence, the English designation of a corporation, "Ltd.," (limited) after a company's name gives notice to the world that those extending credit to it are limited to the corporation's assets to satisfy their claims. In the United States, although "Ltd." can be used to give notice of incorporation, the abbreviation, "Inc.," is more widely used.

Incorporation statutes require the corporation to have both a set of rules that govern the running of the corporation (the by-laws) and a board of directors, which is responsible for setting policy and seeing that their policy is carried out. As a statutory minimum, most states' statutes of incorporation require that the board of directors meet at least once a year. They can meet more often if they choose.

Until recently, hospital boards of directors did not have physicians on them. Either the hospital administrator acted as a conduit between the hospital board and the organized medical staff or there was a liaison committee made up of members from both the board and the medical staff. Today, there is a trend toward having physicians on hospital boards. They are chosen for the same reasons other directors are and not solely because they are physicians.

The chief administrative officer directs the day to day running of a corporation and is responsible to the board of directors. In the past, the chief administrative officer was often a physician or a nurse; today, the hospital administrator is more than likely a business executive trained for the job. In addition to reporting to the board of directors, the hospital administrator confers with the medical staff, the other professional personnel, the employees, the community, and various governmental agencies that regulate the operation of the hospital.

To summarize: the hospital (1) has a corporate structure just like any other corporation but with the unique addition of an organized medical staff; (2) has a hotel function; (3) offers skilled nursing services and diagnostic facilities; and (4) gives the physician an opportunity to diagnose and treat his patient.

Up to this point, and insofar as the patient and the physician are concerned, the hospital appears to be a passive entity. This is only part of the picture. The hospital as a corporate entity has always had the responsibility for selecting those physicians whom it would permit to use its facilities. Since the vast majority of hospitals are organized not by physicians but by laymen, who also make up the boards of directors, the question arose: should laymen or physicians evaluate, screen, and select the physicians who are extended the privilege of practicing at that hospital? It is universally felt that, although these tasks had to be delegated to physicians, the ultimate responsibility for the choice rested with the hospital as a corporate entity. Therefore, once the hospital has been organized and physicians invited to use its facilities, the hospital must necessarily delegate to those invited physicians the authority to select other physicians who will be admitted to practice within it, and to retain the heretofore inchoate responsibility of monitoring the level of medical care. Even though necessity dictates that the hospital delegate its authority to select and monitor those physicians who practice within it, the hospital is still charged with the responsibility for that selection and monitoring.

Once granted the privilege of practicing at the hospital, physicians have found it useful to organize themselves into a more or less formal unit. The complexity of the medical staff's organization depends upon how large the staff is. The smaller it is, the more informal its organization is likely to be. The larger the medical staff, the more organized it is likely to be; in fact, its table of organization may resemble that of a small corporation.

The table of contents of, and selected paragraphs from, Vanderbilt University Hospital's Medical By-Laws, is representative of the rights and duties of a medical staff.

By-Laws of the Medical Staff of Vanderbilt Hospital

Introduction

Preamble

Whereas, the Vanderbilt University is a nonprofit corporation organized under the laws of the State of Tennessee; and whereas one of its activities is to operate a general hospital providing patient care, education and research, and whereas it is recognized that the medical staff is responsible for the quality of medical care in the hospital and must accept and discharge this responsibility to fulfill the hospital's obligations to its patients, subject to the ultimate authority of the Board of Trust; and whereas it is recognized that this responsibility must be carried out with the cooperative efforts of the medical staff, the Executive Director of the Hospital, the Vice President for Medical Affairs, the President, the Chancellor and the governing body;

NOW, THEREFORE, the physicians, dentists and allied staff practicing in this medical center hereby organize themselves into a medical staff in conformity with these by-laws:

DEFINITIONS

1. The term "practitioner" means an appropriately licensed medical physician with an unlimited license or a physician who is otherwise practicing in accordance with the laws of the State of Tennessee, or an appropriately licensed dentist.

2. The term "medical staff" means all medical physicians holding unlimited licenses or who are otherwise practicing in accordance with the laws of the State of Tennessee, and duly licensed dentists and allied staff who are privileged to attend patients in the Vanderbilt University Hospital.

3. The term "Hospital Medical Board" means the committee of the medical staff with representation from all clinical services, and Hospital and medical center administration.

• • •

9. The term "Hospital Committee" means the Vanderbilt University Hospital Committee of the Board of Trust which has been delegated the responsibility to review for the Board of Trust certain matters relating to Vanderbilt University Hospital as defined in the By-laws of the

Vanderbilt Hospital Committee of the Board of Trust.

. . .

11. The Joint Meeting is composed of representatives from the Hospital Committee of the Board of Trust and Medical Staff delegates and Administration and performs the functions of a Joint Committee.

ARTICLES

ARTICLE I: NAME

The name of this organization shall be the Medical Staff of the Vanderbilt University Hospital.

ARTICLE II: PURPOSES

The purpose of the by-laws and rules and regulations of the medical staff shall be:

1. To insure that all patients admitted to or treated in any of the facilities, departments, or services of the hospital shall receive the best possible medical care.
2. To insure a high level of professional performance of all practitioners licensed to practice in the hospital through the appropriate delineation of clinical privileges that each practitioner may exercise in the hospital and through an ongoing review and evaluation of each practitioner's performance in the hospital.
3. To insure the development and maintenance of the highest of educational standards in keeping with the requirements of both undergraduate and graduate medical education, and to maintain scientific standards that will be to the continuous advancement of professional knowledge and skill.
4. To initiate and maintain rules and regulations for self-government of the medical staff; and

5. To provide a means whereby problems of medical practice and medical administration may be considered by the medical staff in consultation with the Executive Director of the Hospital, the Vice President for Medical Affairs, the President, the Chancellor, the Board of Trust, and to provide a means of communication among these groups.

ARTICLE III: MEDICAL STAFF MEMBERSHIP

Section 1 Nature of Medical Staff Membership
Section 2 Qualifications for Membership
Section 3 Conditions and Duration of Appointment

ARTICLE IV: CATEGORIES OF THE MEDICAL STAFF

Section 1 The Active Staff
Section 2 The Associate Staff
Section 3 The Visiting Staff
Section 4 The Resident Staff
Section 5 The Consulting Staff
Section 6 The Emeritus Staff
Section 7 The Honorary Staff

ARTICLE V: THE ALLIED STAFF

Section 1 Definition of Allied Staff

a. The Allied Staff consists of those health care professionals who participate in the diagnostic evaluation and therapy of patients under the direction of a duly licensed physician or dentist. They must be appointed to a service and must have definite lines of supervision made a part of the application. The Allied Staff members are not eligible to vote or to hold offices.
Section 2 Mechanism for Appointment
Section 3 Processing the Applications

of the Board of Trust and Medical Staff Delegates (hereinafter referred to as "Joint Committee") shall consist of the following:

(1) selected representatives of the medical staff chosen by the Hospital Medical Board or its Executive Committee;

(2) the current chairperson and deputy chairperson and immediate past chairperson and deputy chairperson of the Hospital Medical Board;

(3) the members of the Hospital Committee of the Board of Trust;

(4) the Executive Director of the Hospital;

(5) the Dean of the School of Medicine;

(6) the Vice President for Medical Affairs.

b. The purpose of the Joint Meeting shall be to provide for official liaison and closer coordination among the medical staff, the governing body and administration. Meetings of this body will serve as a forum for the expression and discussion of ideas, goals, plans and problems of the medical staff; the members will discuss and interpret issues, comments and recommendations of mutual interest, both at the Joint Meeting and at meetings of their respective bodies where their informed comments will facilitate better understanding and further discussion. The agenda for the Joint Meeting will be set by the medical staff. The Joint Meeting may hear also actions against medico-administrative personnel as set forth in Article VIII, Section 3, and may act as a special mediating board when the need arises.

c. The Joint Meeting shall meet quarterly or as often as needed to effect satisfactory medical-administration-governing body liaison. Any of the following may call a Joint Meeting: the Hospital Medical Board or its Executive Committee; the Vice President for Medical Affairs; the President; the Chancellor; or the Hospital Committee. A permanent record of its meetings will be maintained. Attendance at regular and special Joint Meetings shall be limited to members and such guests as a majority of the members present vote to admit.

ARTICLE XI: CLINICAL SERVICES

Section 1 The Clinical Services—Organization and Definitions
Section 2 Qualifications and Selection of Clinical Service Chiefs
Section 3 Functions of the Clinical Chiefs
Section 4 Functions of Clinical Services

ARTICLE XII: COMMITTEES

Section 1 Committees of the Medical Staff
Section 2 Membership on Committees
Section 3 Minutes and Frequency of Committee Meetings
Section 4 Officers of Committees
Section 5 Duties of the Standing Committees

ARTICLE XIII: AMENDMENTS

Proposed amendments to these by-laws may be initiated by the Hospital Medical Board. Proposals for amendment may be acted upon at the next regular meeting after notice given at any regular meeting of the Hospital Medical Board or notice by mail at least two (2) weeks prior to the meeting. It shall require a two-thirds (⅔) majority of the members of the Hospital Medical Board present and voting for adoption. Amendments so initiated shall become effective when approved by the Board of Trust of Vanderbilt University, its Executive Committee, or its Hospital Committee.

• • •

ARTICLE XIV: ADOPTION

• • •

Comment on the By-Laws

The concepts incorporated in the preamble and definitions of the by-laws are clear. How does this section enlarge or diminish the legal standard of care enunciated by the courts? How does one define "best"? What do you think the reasons are for putting in Article V: Allied Staff? Note that Article VI, which has to do with appointments and reappointments, has three sections; while Articles VII, VIII, and IX have a total of thirteen sections dealing with discipline, hearings, and their review for adverse decisions, i.e., due process. Where did the impetus come from for this expenditure of detail? How do you interpret Article X, section 3.b.: "The purpose of the Joint Meeting shall be to provide for official liaison and closer coordination among the medical staff, the governing body and administration...."? The comparative, closer, is used; closer than what? How would you draft the same section?

Malpractice cases make it abundantly clear how society feels the physician should conduct his practice. The following cases make it clear how the courts feel hospitals should behave in processing medical staff appointments.

Case Reports

MIZELL v. NORTH BROWARD HOSPITAL DISTRICT
175 So. 2d 583 (Fla. 1965)
No. 5837

SHANNON, Judge.

Petitioner-complainant originally sought review of an administrative hearing in the circuit court by writ of certiorari. After his petition was dismissed by that court he sought similar relief here. The issue raised is whether there was substantial evidence supporting the North Broward Hospital District's Board of Commissioners suspension of petitioner's surgical privileges in the hospitals within their jurisdiction.

• • •

Not every member of the hospital's medical staff is allowed to practice surgery. Surgical privileges in varying degree are granted only to those who demonstrate special training and experience in the field of surgery. The

petitioner had previously qualified under the rules of
Provident Hospital to practice general (unlimited) surgery.
The continuation of such privileges, and indeed staff membership itself, was subject to the annual review and reap-
proval by the board of commissioners of the respondent
district. On July 19, 1961, the memberships and privileges
of all members of the medical staff were submitted to the
board of commissioners of the respondent district for
annual review and re-appointment. Concurrent with the
request for re-appointment to membership and privileges
the board of commissioners received a report from the district pathologist indicating that an unreasonably high percentage of normal tissue was removed in appendectomies
performed by the petitioner. Pursuant to this report, the
board of commissioners refused to renew the petitioner's
surgical privileges, and so advised the petitioner. The petitioner then filed this action in the circuit court, seeking,
among other relief, an order delaying further administrative action by the board of commissioners. The board was
temporarily enjoined in order that the petitioner might
have an opportunity to prepare for an administrative hearing concerning the suspension of these privileges. Subsequently a hearing was held by the board of commissioners
during which the petitioner was given an opportunity to
cross-examine witnesses and introduce evidence in his own
behalf. Following the hearing the board made findings of
fact, pursuant to which the earlier action suspending
petitioner's surgical privileges in the district's hospitals was
affirmed.

• • •

Petitioner's attack centers around two main points,
which are: (1) that the original summary proceeding suspending his surgical privileges was a denial of procedural
due process; and (2) there was not sufficient competent
evidence before the board to justify its finding that the
original suspension should be affirmed.

In considering the first point, we notice that: (a) the issue
came before the board of commissioners as a part of

annual approval for medical staff membership and privileges for the coming year; (b) in reaching a determination upon this issue the board of commissioners had before it a request for staff approval from Provident Hospital and a report from the district pathologist indicating that three physicans requesting re-appointment had far exceeded the reasonable limits of normal tissue removal; (c) the board of commissioners suspended any further surgical privileges by these three physicians, but at the same time offered to them, privately and without notoriety, the reasons for the action and offered to them a future hearing before the board of commissioners if they so desired; and (d) the board provided a month's time period for the doctors concerned to conclude their pending surgical practice and to avail themselves of this opportunity for a hearing before their suspension would be effective.

[1,2] A physician's use of a public hospital has been held by the courts of the State of Florida to be a privilege rather than a right, and to be less strictly protected by the provisions of due process than that of an unqualified right [citation omitted]. This physician either knew or should have known the standards which his profession required of his practice within the limits of the district. It is within every reasonable application of due process that summary proceedings be available to protect the hospital and its patients whenever it shall appear from evidence of almost precise mathematical certainty these standards are being negligently or wilfully violated [citations omitted].

[3] The sequence of events in which suspension preceded hearing does not, in itself, violate due process when other procedural standards are satisfied. This is especially true when countervailing interests of the protection of hospital patients are considered. . . .

[4,5] In considering petitioner's second point regarding the hearing itself, we have examined the record and found substantial evidence supporting the board's findings of fact. Included in the evidence presented was testimony of the district pathologist, testimony of a practicing surgeon, and a case by case analysis of the medical reports on patients having normal tissue removed by petitioner. The witnesses testified that post-operative microscopic exami-

nation of removed appendixes is the method used to confirm a preliminary diagnosis of acute appendicitis. They further testified that when other symptoms are present, the diagnosis of appendicitis is not fairly chargeable against a surgeon, and for that reason considerable leeway, up to thirty-five percent, of mistaken diagnosis is allowed. Examination of tissue removed from petitioner's patients indicated mistaken diagnosis in seventy per cent of his appendectomies, which figure far exceeded normal allowable limitations. In light of this testimony, we are convinced that there was competent substantial evidence before the board which supported its findings of fact. In petitions for certiorari, this is the limit of a court's power of review [citation omitted]. Where findings of fact by an administrative agency are supported by the evidence, the court cannot substitute its own findings [citation omitted].

[6] We are also convinced that the procedural requirements of due process regarding the conduct of the hearing were met. Petitioner was accorded adequate notice and availed himself of the opportunity to cross-examine witnesses and present evidence in his own behalf. . . .

We have thoroughly considered the record in this case and have no hesitation in saying that the evidence goes far beyond the substantial evidence rule by which we are bound in a petition for certiorari.[1]

Certiorari is denied.

ALLEN, Acting C. J., and WHITE, J., concur.

PETERSON v. TUCSON GENERAL HOSPITAL, INC.
114 Ariz. 66 (App.), 559 P.2d 186 (1976)
HOWARD, Chief Judge.

Appellant, an osteopathic physician, filed suit against Tucson General Hospital alleging that the hospital wrongfully denied his re-application for staff membership. After depositions were taken and interrogatories answered, the

---

[1]Certiorari is a procedural device in which the highest appellate court certifies to a lower court that the legal issue is of such a grave nature that the highest court will take jurisdiction and hear the case and make a decision.

hospital moved for summary judgment. The superior court granted the motion and appellant appeals.

Appellant was a member of the staff of Tucson General Hospital from 1959 to 1969. The seeds giving rise to the present litigation were planted during the later years of his staff membership when the hospital continually reprimanded appellant and eventually revoked his staff privileges for his refusal to follow the hospital's rules and regulations.

In May 1972 appellant re-applied for membership on the staff of Tucson General Hospital. Although the credentials committee and the department of general practice recommended the acceptance of appellant's application the executive committee recommended that staff privileges be denied ". . . in view of past performance which was not acceptable. . . ." When appellant was notified of the executive committee's recommendation, he requested a hearing before an ad hoc committee of the staff, as provided for in the hospital's bylaws. The committee was appointed and a hearing was held in March of 1973. The ad hoc committee upheld the recommendation of the executive committee to deny privileges on the following grounds:

> "1. Dr. Peterson has given us no reason to believe he would, or wanted to practice on the staff.
> 2. We have no assurance that Dr. Peterson would abide by the rules and regulations of Tucson General Hospital in the future.
> 3. We have not received a reply to our letter to the Benson Hospital which had requested further information regarding Dr. Sherman Peterson."

Appellant then appealed the decision of the ad hoc committee of the staff to the Board of Trustees which pursuant to the bylaws was to act in an appellate capacity. The Board of Trustees found that there was evidence to support the committee's findings and upheld the decision.

Appellant claims that the hospital's refusal to grant him staff privileges was wrongful because (1) the hospital failed to adopt proper standards for making the determination, (2) the hospital's action was arbitrary and capricious as a matter of law because the board considered his past conduct and (3) the hospital did not treat appellant's application the same as those of other osteopaths who were granted privileges. He further asserts there were factual disputes which precluded the granting of summary judgment.

[1–4] The threshold question which must be answered is when are the rules and acts of a hospital subject to judicial review? The answer depends upon whether the hospital is private, public, or "quasi public". The principal distinguishing feature of a private hospital is that it has the power to manage its own affairs and is not subject to the direct control of a governmental agency. [Citation omitted.] The public hospital is an instrumentality of the state, founded and owned in the public interest, supported by public funds, and governed by those deriving their authority from the state. A "quasi public" status is achieved if what otherwise would be a truly private hospital was constructed with public funds, is presently receiving public benefits or has been sufficiently incorporated into a governmental plan for providing hospital facilities to the public.[Citation omitted.]

[5,6] The general rule is that the exclusion of a physician from staff privileges in a private hospital is a matter which ordinarily rests within the discretion of the managing authorities thereof, not subject to judicial review. [Citations omitted.] This general rule does not apply where there is a contention that the hospital failed to conform to procedural requirements set forth in a hospital's constitution, bylaws, or rules and regulations. [Citation omitted.]

[7] There is no doubt that as far as public hospitals are concerned the Fourteenth Amendment of the United States Constitution applies and constitutional rights will be enforced by the courts. [Citation omitted.]

A growing number of courts have subjected hospital bylaws, constitutions, acts and rules and regulations to judicial scrutiny based upon the definition of "quasi public" set forth in [Citation omitted], or on the basis of common law. In *Greisman v. Newcomb Hospital*, 40 N.J. 389, 192 A.2d 817 (1963) the court was concerned with the validity of a hospital bylaw forbidding staff privileges to osteopaths.

The plaintiff, an osteopath, had an unrestricted license to practice medicine in the state of New Jersey. He practiced medicine in Vineland which had a population of 10,000. There was only one hospital in Vineland. The judicial council of the medical society of the State of New Jersey had adopted a resolution which declared that it would not be unethical for members to enter into professional association with any person holding a full license as a physician or a surgeon granted by the state board of examiners who adheres to the scientific principles of the American Medical Association and the New Jersey Medical Society. Other hospitals in the area had admitted osteopathic physicians to their medical staff.

The hospital sought to prevent judicial intervention on the grounds that it was a private hospital. The court, however, held the bylaw to be invalid. Although the court noted that the hospital was a non-profit organization and received a good measure of its funds from public sources and through public solicitation, its decision was based upon other grounds. The court first pointed out that the hospital constituted a virtual monopoly in the area. It then showed how activities which were much less public, such as innkeepers, carriers, etc., had been made subject to judicial scrutiny for the common good since they were "affected with the public interest." The court in *Greisman* relied most heavily upon its prior decision in *Falcone v. Middlesex County Medical Society*, 34 N.J. 582, 170 A.2d 791 (1961) where it struck down an arbitrary membership requirement in the Middlesex County Medical Society. In *Falcone* it had characterized the society as an organization engaged in an activity of public concern and found its power was not unbridled but was to be viewed judicially as a fiduciary power to be exercised in a reasonable and lawful manner for the advancement of the interest of the medical profession and the public generally. The *Greisman* court stated that although *Falcone* was concerned with a medical society rather than a hospital, similar policy considerations apply with equal strength and call for a declaration that the hospital's power to pass on staff membership applications is a fiduciary one since the hospital is publicly dedicated primarily to the sick and

injured of Vineland and its vicinity and the public expects
its doctors to be able to use that facility.

In the case of *Sussman v. Overlook Hospital Association*, 95 N.J. Super. 418, 231 A.2d 289 (1967) the court
followed *Greisman* stating that the board of trustees of a
private hospital, private in the sense that it is non-
governmental, does have the right to reject an applicant
for staff privileges so long as it acts in a fair manner and for
a valid reason. The court observed that a board of trustees
may reasonably consider the factor of prospective
disharmony. It further stated that while the board should
provide the applicant an opportunity to appeal and present
witnesses, it is not essential that he be afforded the rights of
cross-examination or to be represented by counsel. All that
is required is for the board to be fully informed so that it
may make an intelligent, reasonable judgment in good
faith upon all the facts presented.

. . .

California [citation omitted] adopted the *Falcone*
rationale in a case involving admittance to a private medical society. In addition to a requirement that the decision
of the society be reasonable and not arbitrary or capricious, the court held that an application for membership
was to be decided pursuant to the common law
requirement of "fair procedure". It termed "fair procedure"
as that which provides the applicant with adequate notice
of the "charges" against him and a reasonable opportunity
to respond.

In some cases receipt of federal funding has resulted in
the right to judicial review based on the fact that the hospital is "quasi public". Thus in *Silver v. Castle Memorial
Hospital*, supra, the hospital was private but received con-
tributions of funds under the Hill-Burton Act of 1965, 42
U.S.C. Sec. 291, in addition to state funds. The court sanc-
tioned judicial review but carefully limited its opinion to
those situations where the hospital has more than nominal
government involvement in the form of funding. Other
courts have rejected this concept. [Citation omitted.]

. . . In the case of *Blende v. Maricopa County Medical*

Society, 96 Ariz. 240, 393 P.2d 926 (1964) the court agreed with the reasoning in *Falcone*. [Footnote omitted.] The appellant was denied membership in the Maricopa County Medical Society. This resulted in the prevention of his maintenance of staff privileges in the hospitals of Maricopa County since the right to staff privileges depended upon membership in the society. In justifying judicial intervention the court stated:

> "The interests in freedom of association and in autonomy for private associations make it desirable to allow private groups to determine their own membership. But when a medical society controls a doctor's access to hospital facilities, then the society's exercise of a quasi-governmental power is the legitimate object of judicial concern." 96 Ariz. at 244, 393 P.2d at 929.

[8,9] It is clear that the policy considerations in *Blende* are equally applicable here. Tucson General Hospital is the only osteopathic hospital in Tucson and thus constitutes a virtual monopoly since it is the only hospital in which an osteopathic physician may have staff privileges. We conclude that judicial review is proper. Our review, however, is not broad but is limited. If the hospital has refused staff privileges on the basis of factual findings supported by substantial evidence and reached its decision by the application of a reasonable standard, i.e. one that comports with the legitimate goals of the hospital and the rights of the individual and the public, then judicial inquiry should end. [Citation omitted.]

[10] Appellant claims that the hospital had not adopted standards for evaluating his application for staff privileges. The hospital asserts that the relevant criteria for his case are reflected in the findings of the ad hoc committee: (1) the applicant must desire to practice in the hospital; and (2) the applicant must demonstrate a willingness to follow the rules and regulations. We agree with the hospital.

Are there genuine issues of fact which preclude summary judgment? The depositions and an affidavit filed by the hospital in support of its motion for summary judgment show that prior to the withdrawal of his staff privileges in 1969 there was a long history of confrontations between Dr. Peterson and the staff concerning rules and regulations such as failing to keep records up-to-date and failing to seek consultation when consultation should have been required. There was also an issue as to the quality of medical care that he afforded the patients. This led to the signing of written agreements with the hospital that he would follow the rules and regulations but when he failed to do so, his staff privileges were withdrawn. Members of the board of trustees and the ad hoc committee asserted that Dr. Peterson would give them no unequivocal assurance that if his privileges were reinstated he would abide by the rules and regulations of the hospital. They also stated that Dr. Peterson led them to believe that if his privileges were reinstated he did not intend to use those privileges but wanted the reinstatement for other reasons.

Dr. Peterson, in his deposition, stated that the reason for his original dismissal was a failure to keep up with hospital records but that many members of the staff were not able to do so yet their privileges were not withdrawn. He further claimed that he told the executive committee that he was willing to follow the rules and regulations of the hospital. As far as staff privileges were concerned, he said he told the committee that he might never put another patient in the hospital but he did not want over 30 years of medicine to "go down the drain". He stated that he did not emphasize the fact that he was not going to use the hospital facilities.

[11] ... In the light of the responsibility of a hospital to supervise the quality of patient care and the legal liability which may result from a failure to screen and supervise its members, a hospital must be allowed broad discretion in evaluating applications for admission to staff. [Citation omitted.]

[12–14] If we resolve all alleged factual disputes in the appellant's favor, summary judgment was still proper. Assuming that he did tell the executive committee and the ad hoc committee that he would follow the rules and regulations of the hospital, that he wanted the restoration of staff privileges in order to clear his record, and that his staff privileges were originally withdrawn for failure to keep proper hospital records, we are still left with the undisputed fact that his privileges were withdrawn for failure to maintain proper records in spite of assurances and written agreements to do so. We cannot say that the maintenance of proper hospital records is unimportant in the care and treatment of patients and the proper administration of a hospital. Considering his past conduct in this regard the board could have reasonably refused staff privileges on this ground alone. The fact that others who are guilty of the same conduct have not been held accountable is of no significance here. [Citation omitted.]

[15] There is nothing in the record that demonstrates the hospital did not treat appellant's application the same as those of other osteopaths who had been granted staff privileges. The only difference in the processing of his application was the consideration of his past conduct while on the staff. His past conduct was pertinent to the board's consideration of whether staff privileges should again be granted.

[16–18] As the court noted in *Sosa v. Board of Managers of Val Verde Memorial Hospital*, 437 F.2d 173 (5th Cir. 1971):

> "The evaluation of professional proficiency of doctors is best left to the specialized expertise of their peers, subject only to limited judicial surveillance. The court is charged with the narrow responsibility of assuring that the qualifications imposed by the Board are reasonably related to the operation of the hospital and fairly administered. In short, so long as staff selections are administered with fairness, geared by a rationale compatible with hospital responsibility, and unencumbered with irrelevant considerations, a court should not interfere." 437 F.2d at 177.

Affirmed.
KRUCKER and HATHAWAY, JJ., concur.

The Hospital as Watchdog of Medical Care

The following recent cases show how our society, speaking through its courts, perceives the dimensions of the hospital's responsibility to the patient vis-a-vis the physician's care.

Read the *Corleto, Joiner, Purcell, Misevch,* and *Pederson* cases in the light of the question: if the hospital has these responsibilities, what are its accompanying rights?

CORLETO v. SHORE MEMORIAL HOSPITAL
138 N.J. Super. 302, 350 A.2d 534 (1975)

MANUEL H. GREENBERG, J.C.C., Temporarily Assigned. Plaintiffs' amended complaint sets forth that their decedent was subjected to malpractice on the part of defendant Dr. Josiah Calvin McCracken, Jr., while a patient in defendant hospital, leading to her death. In addition to setting forth a claim against the doctor, claim is also made against the hospital as well as the administrator, board of directors and the medical staff thereof on the ground that they knew or should have known that Dr. McCracken was not competent to perform the surgical procedure on the decedent which he did, but they nevertheless permitted him to do so and allowed him to remain on the case when the situation was obviously beyond his control.

Defendants hospital, administrator, board of directors and medical staff have moved to dismiss the amended complaint for failure to state a claim upon which relief can be granted. . . .

The amended complaint alleges in substance, among other things, that *the board of directors and administrator* had a duty to provide and maintain competent medical personnel for patients at the hospital and to admit and allow only those physicians duly qualified and competent to exercise and have privileges at the hospital; that *the medical staff* had the duty to investigate and then recommend that only licensed, capable and qualified physicians exercise the various privileges at the hospital; that those defendants knew or should have known *by the exercise of reasonable care and diligence* that Dr. McCracken was not competent to perform the abdominal surgery that he performed on plaintiffs' decedent; that they nevertheless permitted and allowed him to carry out the surgery and, moreover, allowed him to remain on the case when it was obvious that the situation had gone completely beyond his control and competence, and that the negligence of said defendants directly contributed to the plaintiffs' damages. [Italics added.]

... Here ... the moving defendants are charged with wrongdoing separate and distinct from that of Dr. McCracken, albeit that plaintiffs would obviously have to establish wrongdoing on the part of that doctor in order to prevail against the other defendants.

● ● ●

... It needs no citation of authority to state that, in general, where one is charged with liability for the negligence of another it is a good defense that the person doing the ultimate harm was an independent contractor rather than an employee of the one sought to be charged. However, certain exceptions have come to be accepted, one of which is that if a person engages an incompetent contractor he may be held liable for the ultimate damage caused by such contractor. [Citation omitted.] ... Liability does not attach vicariously but because of the wrongful act in placing an incompetent in a position to do harm. This, in essence, is what plaintiffs now contend. ...

Turning to other jurisdictions which have considered the same or similar questions as those involved herein, the case of *Hull v. North Valley Hospital,* 159 *Mont.* 375, 498 *P.*2d 136 (Sup. Ct. 1972), is on point. Plaintiff was treated by his family physician at defendant hospital. His condition worsened and suit was instituted against the hospital for its negligence under the ordinary rules of negligence in permitting the doctor to practice within it. The court expressed the central issue thus (at 143): "Is the Hospital negligent under the ordinary rules of negligence for not limiting or expelling the doctor *before the fact* of the case of malpractice, and excluding any reference to the malpractice itself except in damages?" Thereafter the court answered its question as follows:

At the risk of belabored definition, the integration

of a modern hospital becomes readily apparent as the
various boards, reviewing committees, and designation of privileges are found to rest on a structure
designed to control, supervise, and review the work
within the hospital. The standards of hospital accreditation, the state licensing regulations, and the respondent's bylaws demonstrate that the medical profession and other responsible authorities regard it
as both desirable and feasible that a hospital assume
certain responsibilities for the care of the patient. [at
143.]

. . . [T]he Montana court was quite willing to find an independent duty of care running from the hospital to the
patient.

• • •

The case of *Fiorentino v. Wenger*, 19 N.Y.2d 407, 280
N.Y.S.2d 373, 227 N.E.2d 296 (Ct. App. 1967), contains
language bearing upon the point in question. The case
involved the death of a patient following a relatively novel
type of operation. The surgeon was selected by the
patient's family and was not a hospital employee. The
court stated that:

It should be evident that a hospital generally cannot be held liable, other than derivatively, for another's malpractice. Thus, where, as here, there is no
vicarious liability, the plaintiff must establish that the
hospital, through its own agents, was guilty of
malpractice or other tort concurring in causing the
harm. Where a hospital's alleged misconduct
involves an omission to act, the hospital will not be
held responsible unless it had reason to know that it
should have acted within the duty it concededly had.
***More particularly, in the context of the present
case, a hospital will not be held liable for an act of
malpractice performed by an independently retained
healer, unless it had reason to know that the act of
malpractice would take place.*** [280 N.Y.S.2d at
378, 277 N.E.2d at 299]

The court went on to conclude that unless it could be said
that the performance of the type of operation in question
were *per se* an act of malpractice, the hospital could not be
held liable. However, if we apply the reasoning of *Fiorentino* to the case at bar it seems clear, assuming that the allegations of the amended complaint are substantiated, that
the permitting of an operation by one known to be incompetent to perform it, as well as the failure to remove him
from the case when problems have become obvious, would
be a basis upon which to impose liability on those responsible.

•   •   •

. . . The argument is made that the public good can best
be served by not subjecting every hospital administrator,
director or trustee and medical staff member in the State to
the constant threat of a lawsuit whenever it is alleged that
negligence occurred in a hospital. . . . The public policy arguments advanced for granting the moving defendants an
immunity can be countered by other arguments. Thus, it
can be argued that subjecting persons in the class to liability will serve to make them more aware of their responsibilities in assuring that only competent physicians practice within their hospitals, thereby raising the level of
medical care within the State.

•   •   •

. . . The medical staff of the Shore Memorial Hospital, a
group of 141 doctors, named as a defendant, urges that it is
not amenable to suit as an unincorporated association. . . .
This argument is without merit. Plaintiffs could have
named all 141 doctors individually as defendants, but to
do so would serve no useful purpose. The law permitting
suits against unincorporated associations is remedial legislation and is to be given as liberal an interpretation as possible, consistent with its language. [Citation omitted.]
There is precedent for designating the medical staff of a
hospital as a party in a civil action. [Citations omitted.]
For the reasons stated above the motion will be denied.

MITCHELL COUNTY HOSPITAL AUTHORITY v. JOINER
229 Ga. 140, 189 S.E.2d 412 (1972)

NICHOLS, Justice. Certiorari was granted in this case to review the decision of the Court of Appeals with respect to the responsibility of a Hospital Authority in permitting an unqualified physician to serve on its staff, although such physician holds a valid license from the State of Georgia to practice medicine.

The applicant, Hospital Authority, cites in support of its application for certiorari cases wherein it has been held that a hospital is not responsible in damages for the negligent or unskilful treatment by a surgeon or physician employed on its staff where it has exercised reasonable care in the selection of a physician or surgeon and selects an authorized physician in good standing in his profession. [Citation omitted.] [Case], also relied upon by the applicant, relates to a situation where the Hospital Authority does not, and has no authority to, exercise any control in the diagnosis or treatment of the illness or injury. Such rule is generally recognized throughout the country. . . .

The present case, however, does not come within the above cited authorities, for the plaintiff does not seek to hold the Hospital Authority liable under the doctrine of respondeat superior or principal and agent, but upon the doctrine of independent negligence in permitting the alleged negligent physician to practice his profession in the hospital, when his incompetency is known. . . .

In *Yeargin v. Hamilton Memorial Hospital*, 225 Ga. 661 (171 SE2d 136), it was held: "The court did not err in holding that the Hospital Authority was not required to grant a physician unlimited and unrestricted rights to serve as a member of the active staff of the hospital operated by the Authority, and not required to allow him to use all of the privileges of active staff members according to the dictates of his own opinion and judgment. The Authority and hospital may restrict a staff member's privileges by reasonable and nondiscriminatory rules and regulations." It was recognized in that opinion that the Hospital Authority had authority to limit the practice by physicians to those procedures which it deems such physician qualified to perform.

In *Dunbar v. Hospital Authority of Gwinnett County*, 227 Ga. 534 (182 SE2d 89), with one Justice dissenting, it was held that a physician could be barred from practicing medicine in the hospitals operated by the Authority where he did not comply with various rules of the Authority.

These two cases require a finding that a Hospital Authority operating a public hospital has authority *to examine* the qualifications of any physician seeking staff privileges and *to limit* his practice to those areas in which he is deemed qualified to practice or *to completely bar* him from such practice if he is incompetent, unqualified, inexperienced or reckless. [Italics added.]

... [T]he delegation of the authority to screen applicants for staff membership on the medical staff does not relieve the Authority of its responsibility, since the members of such staff act as agents for the Authority, and whether it knew or from the information in its possession the incompetency of the physician was known, is a question of fact. If the physician was incompetent and the Authority knew, or from information in its possession such incompetency was apparent, then it cannot be said that the Authority acted in good faith and with reasonable care in permitting the physician to become a member of its staff.

The affidavit in support of the motion for summary judgment did not pierce the allegations of the plaintiff's complaint and the judgment of the Court of Appeals reversing the grant of such motion was not error for any reason assigned.

Judgment affirmed....

PURCELL and TUCSON GENERAL HOSPITAL v. ZIMBELMAN
18 Ariz. App. 75, 500 P.2d 335 (1972)

HOWARD, Judge.

This was an action for negligence against a hospital and several doctors. Prior to submission to the jury, all doctors were dismissed from the action except Dr. Purcell.

The jury returned a $150,000 verdict against both the hospital and Dr. Purcell. In this appeal the hospital presents the following questions:

"1. In order to prove a prima facie case, must the plaintiff prove that defendant's alleged negligence caused injury to the plaintiff? Specifically, in this case, was the plaintiff required to prove that the hospital's alleged negligence in failing to restrict or supervise Dr. Purcell after the Blickley and Hill cases resulted in the injury to the plaintiff?

2. Even though it may be proper to introduce into evidence the fact that a doctor has been sued on two previous occasions for malpractice on the issue of whether or not a hospital had notice of the doctor's possible incompetency, is it proper to advise the jury of every fact and circumstance of those lawsuits including the judgments rendered, and is it further proper to introduce into evidence two other lawsuits which have nothing to do with the disease or treatment at issue in the instant case, and in which there is no evidence that the doctor was guilty of professional negligence?

• • •

7. What is the duty of a hospital toward its patients? Is it liable for the negligence of physicians who are not employees but are on its staff, and acting as staff members or committee members? Is a hospital liable for the failures of its surgical staff if it does not have reason to know that the surgical staff is not policing itself properly?"

• • •

The facts considered in the light most favorable to support the verdict are as follows.

In April of 1969, Henry Zimbelman, 62 years of age, began having trouble with his bowels. He went to an osteopathic general surgeon who found an obstruction in the descending colon and admitted Zimbelman to Tucson General Hospital on April 14, 1969. Dr. Coy Purcell, a general surgeon, was asked to consult. Purcell's initial diagnosis was that Zimbelman had either cancer or diverticulitis of the lower large bowel. The trouble in Zimbelman's case was located above the peritoneal reflection. A barium enema x-ray report showed a complete obstruction in the area of the rectosigmoid junction. [All Footnotes omitted.]

Zimbelman was also given a sigmoidscopic examination by Purcell which consists of the insertion of a tube-like instrument called a sigmoidscope through the anus, up the rectum and into the colon. According to the testimony of Purcell the sigmoidscope passed 17 cm. from the outlet of the anus, which meant that it passed through the entire rectum, through the peritoneal reflection and into the rectosigmoid junction. This means that the diseased portion of the bowel was located at least 17 cm. above the outlet of the anus.

On April 18, 1969, Purcell operated on Zimbelman and found a lesion running circularly around the rectosigmoid colon. Since Purcell could not tell by sight whether the lesion was cancerous he had a pathologist come into the operating room to look at the tissue. Although surgical standards require the surgeon to obtain a frozen section, relying on the pathologist who said the lesion looked like cancer, Purcell performed a "cancer operation" called a "Babcock-Bacon proctosigmoidectomy." This procedure was first described by and is named after Drs. Babcock and Bacon and is also called a "pull-through" operation.

In doing the "pull-through" Purcell first opened the abdomen and removed a piece of the bowel. The uppermost portion of what was removed was three inches above the point of the lesion. Purcell then took the end of the remaining bowel (called the proximal end) and "pulled it through" the peritoneal reflection into the rectum, where he attached it at the anus. All of the bowel and rectum below the proximal end of the resection were thus discarded. Purcell did not first institute a temporary colostomy because he did not think it was necessary, even though there had been contamination of this proximal end before he pulled it through into the rectal area and attached it to the anal outlet and even though he knew there had been an infectious process in the abdomen.

Purcell testified that he could not have performed an anterior resection on Zimbelman because the lesion was low down in a cylindrical pelvis, he had an inadequate cuff and had no room to work.

As a result of the "pull-through" operation Zimbelman suffered from loss of sexual functions, loss of a kidney, a permanent colostomy and urinary problems.

Dr. Griess, the former chief of staff at St. Mary's hospital in Tucson, testified that the choice of treatment on Zimbelman should have been an anterior resection and not a "pull-through." Dr. Clements testified that Purcell's failure to perform an anterior resection fell below the standard of the average competent bowel surgeon. The surgeons were relatively unanimous in the opinion that a "pull-through" was an operation designed only for disease located below the peritoneal reflection and that where, as in Zimbelman's case, the problem is located above the peritoneal reflection, even if low-down, there is no indication for doing a "pull-through."

Dr. Clements testified that the inherent risks of a "pull-through," especially one performed without a diverting colostomy, are high.

The court admitted testimony concerning two patients who were treated by Purcell prior to Zimbelman. Francis Blickley was treated by Purcell in 1965 for a condition which Purcell suspected of being either cancer or diverticulitis of the lower portion of the colon.

One year later Purcell treated a Hattie Hill for a condition which Purcell suspected of being either cancer or diverticulitis of the colon.

Both were cases of diverticulitis and in neither case did Purcell perform an anterior resection. Blickley and Hill were later treated by Dr. Griess for complications resulting from Purcell's treatment. Dr. Griess performed an anterior resection on Blickley and was eventually able to restore bowel continuity.

Dr. Griess attempted to perform an anterior resection on Hattie Hill but he was unable to do so because of her prior treatment. As a result of Purcell's failure to perform an anterior resection on Mrs. Hill she was left with a permanent colostomy.

Both Hill and Blickley sued Purcell and the hospital. Two other patients of Dr. Purcell sued Purcell and the hospital. All suits occurred prior to Purcell's treatment of Zimbelman.

NEGLIGENCE OF THE HOSPITAL

Zimbelman's theory against the hospital was that the hospital had a duty to the public to allow the use of its facilities only by such independent staff doctors as are professionally competent and who treat their patients in full accordance with accepted and established medical practices, and that the hospital breached its duty when it failed to take any action against Purcell when it knew, or should have known, that he lacked the skill to treat the condition in question.

The hospital claimed that it could not be liable for Purcell's malpractice since he was an independent contractor and there was no reason to believe that a specific act of malpractice would take place.

The hospital has been accredited by the American Osteopathic Association. In order to be accredited by that association in the first instance and in order to maintain its accreditation, the association requires that the governing body of the hospital, to wit the board of trustees, be properly organized and mandates that this governing body must have the ultimate responsibility for the quality of patient care rendered in the hospital. In addition, the association requires creation of a professional staff. According to the Basic Accreditation Requirements of the American Osteopathic Association, the following is required:

> "The governing authorities of the hospital have a responsibility of selecting its professional staff to assure the community that the physician to whom it extends the privilege of the use of its facilities are professionally competent and will offer optimum patient care. . . ."

Pursuant to the requirements of the association, a professional staff was created at the hospital. By-Laws, approved by the board of trustees of the hospital state:

> "Fully recognizing that the governing authority of any hospital serving the public has not only the right, but, also the responsibility in selecting its professional Staff to assure itself, and through it the public, that the doctors to whom it extends the privileges to the use of its facilities are professionally competent and ethically sound, and that such governing authority of the hospital has a moral, as well as a legal, obligation toward the patient, the recognition of which enables the person requiring hospital care to enter the institution confident that the treatment he or she will receive there will be in full accordance with accepted and established practice, the Professional Staff of the Tucson General Hospital, Osteopathic, sets out the following purpose: . . ."

The evidence further established that it was the practice among hospitals all over the country to establish and operate review and other committees for the purpose of regulating the privileges granted staff doctors and to insure that privileges are conferred only for those procedures for which the doctor was trained and qualified. Doctor Griess testified that the custom and practice among hospitals was to actually monitor and review the performance of staff doctors and to restrict or suspend their privileges or require supervision when such doctors have demonstrated an inability to handle a certain type of problem.

[1, 2] Dr. Myers, a member of the board of trustees of the hospital, admitted that the hospital was aware of the custom and practice, subscribed to it and attempted to follow it. In spite of the foregoing, the hospital maintains that since the Blickley and Hill cases were presented to the Department of Surgery, a group of independent doctors on the professional staff, the hospital cannot be liable for the inaction of the surgical department. We are unable to agree with this position. The Basic Accreditation Requirements of the American Osteopathic Association and the By-Laws

of the Professional Staff of Tucson General Hospital approved by the board of trustees of the hospital demonstrate that the osteopathic doctors themselves and other responsible authorities regard as both desirable and feasible that a hospital assume certain responsibilities for the care of its patients. The hospital had assumed the duty of supervising the competence of its staff doctors. The Department of Surgery was acting for and on behalf of the hospital in fulfilling this duty and if the department was negligent in not taking any action against Purcell or recommending to the board of trustees that action be taken, then the hospital would also be negligent. It cannot be gainsaid that it was a jury question as to whether or not the hospital, acting through its Department of Surgery, was negligent.

PROXIMATE CAUSE

The hospital argues that Zimbelman failed to prove that it caused his injuries because there was no showing as to what action the hospital would have taken with respect to Dr. Purcell. It contends that "... if the hospital should have suspended Dr. Purcell in the Hill case, then a suspension could have lasted for a period of six months. Let us assume that the hospital restricted Dr. Purcell for a six-month period and did not let him perform any surgery on diverticulitis during that time. If that had happened, then according to Dr. Griess the hospital would have performed whatever duties to the public that it had. Yet, even if that restriction had taken place, it is still entirely possible and probable that the Zimbelman case would have occurred exactly as it did occur. The Blickley and Hill cases were over in 1965, and therefore a six-month or even a three-year suspension would have been terminated by the time Henry Zimbelman presented himself to Tucson General Hospital."

The hospital further maintains, since after the Hill and Blickley cases Dr. Purcell recognized that the proper way to handle diverticulitis was by anterior resection and had performed some anterior resections, that "... once it would have become clear to any hospital department or committee that a problem in the Hill or Blickley case had been cleared up—that Dr. Purcell now realized that a diseased portion of the bowel must be taken out—then obviously there would have been no reason to continue any such suspension because of the Blickley and Hill cases." We do not agree with the hospital's contention.

[3, 4] An essential element of the plaintiff's cause of action for negligence is that there must be some reasonable connection between the act or omission of the defendant and the damage which the plaintiff has suffered. On the issue of the fact of causation the plaintiff has the burden of proof. He must introduce evidence which affords a reasonable basis for the conclusion that it is more likely than not that the conduct of the defendant was a substantial factor in bringing about the result. This "substantial factor" test has been applied by our Supreme Court to determining whether or not there was causation in fact. [Citations omitted.] Although a mere possibility of such causation is not enough, the plaintiff is not required to prove his case beyond a reasonable doubt and he need not negate entirely the possibility that the defendant's conduct was not a cause. [Citation omitted.] All that is required in negligence cases is for the plaintiff to present probable facts from which negligence and causal relations may be reasonably inferred. [Citation omitted.]

As aptly stated in Prosser, Law of Torts § 41, at 242 (4th ed. 1971):

> ". . . The fact of causation is incapable of mathematical proof, since no man can say with absolute certainty what would have occurred if the defendant had acted otherwise. Proof of what we call the relation of cause and effect, that of necessary antecedent and inevitable consequence, can be nothing more than 'the projection of our habit of expecting certain consequents to follow certain antecedents merely because we had observed these sequences on previous occasions.' If as a matter of ordinary experience a particular act or omission might be expected, under the circumstances, to produce a particular result, and that result in fact has followed, the conclusion may be permissible that the causal relation exists.

... Thus it is everyday experience that unlighted stairs create a danger that someone will fall. Such a condition 'greatly multiplies the chances of accident, and is of a character naturally leading to its occurrence.' When a fat woman tumbles down the steps, it is a reasonable conclusion that it is more likely than not that the bad lighting has played a substantial part in the fall. When a child is drowned in a swimming pool, no one can say with certainty that a lifeguard would have saved him; but the experience of the community permits the conclusion that the absence of the guard played a significant part in the drowning. Such questions are peculiarly for the jury; ... whether reasonable police precautions would have prevented a boy from shooting a plaintiff in the eye with an airgun, are questions on which a court can seldom rule as a matter of law. And whether the defendant's negligence consists of a violation of some statutory safety regulation, or the breach of a plain common law duty of care, the court can scarcely overlook the fact that the injury which has in fact occurred is precisely the sort of thing that proper care on the part of the defendant would be intended to prevent, and accordingly allow a certain liberality to the jury in drawing its conclusion."

We believe it reasonably probable to conclude that had the hospital taken some action against Dr. Purcell, whether in the form of suspension, remonstration, restriction or other means, the surgical procedure utilized in this case would not have been undertaken by the doctor and Mr. Zimbelman would not have been injured.

[5] Since the question of causation in fact is for the trier of fact [citation omitted], the court did not err in submitting it to the jury.

EVIDENCE OF OTHER CLAIMS

The hospital urges that the admission of evidence regarding the Blickley, Hill, Kelly, and Wolford cases was prejudicially erroneous. Specifically, it complains that the jury was permitted to hear that Dr. Purcell had been sued

on four previous occasions, that Mr. Blickley had re-
covered a judgment against Dr. Purcell, that Mrs. Hill had
"won her case" after suing for "six figures or more", and
that the Kelly and Wolford cases had been filed against
both Purcell and the hospital.

[6] Since the negligence of the hospital was predicated
upon failure to perform its obligation to Zimbelman to see
to it that only professionally competent persons were on its
staff, it follows that its knowledge, actual or constructive,
of Dr. Purcell's shortcomings, was an essential element for
consideration in determining whether or not the hospital
exercised reasonable care or had been guilty of negligence.
Where knowledge of a danger is an issue, evidence of the
occurrence of other accidents or injuries from the doing of
a particular act or the employment of a particular method
on occasions prior to the one in question is admissible to
show that the person charged knew or should have known
of the danger therein, provided it is shown that the conditions of the previous occurrences were the same or sub-
stantially similar to those of the one in question. It is not
necessary however, to show that such incidents occurred
under circumstances precisely the same as those of the one
in question – similarity in general character suffices. [Cita-
tion omitted.]

[7, 8] The hospital contends that the evidence of other
past acts was inadmissible in the case at bench because the
alleged act of negligence in Zimbelman's case was not quite
the same as in the Blickley and Hill cases. We do not agree.
In all three cases an anterior resection was required and
was not performed. There was a sufficient similarity in
such conduct so as to make the Blickley and Hill cases admissible as to the hospital. As to the admissibility of the
Kelly and Wolford cases against the hospital, Dr. Griess
testified that untoward results in prior cases would be
sufficient in and of itself to require a hospital to undertake
a review of the records of those incidents. There was evidence that a negligence suit against a doctor would be further grounds which would require a competent hospital to
review the doctor's records. Dr. Griess also testified that
where the hospital was joined in a lawsuit, review of the
doctor's records was even more of a requirement. There-

fore, evidence of the filing of the Hill, Blickley, Kelly and Wolford lawsuits was admissible against the hospital on the question of notice, not only as to the particular type of operation and ailment that was involved, but as to the general competency of Dr. Purcell to continue to be a member of the hospital staff.

The hospital next questions the action of the trial court in allowing into evidence the fact that there was a verdict against Dr. Purcell in the Blickley case and that Hattie Hill had sued for an amount in excess of six figures. One of the hospital's theories of defense was that nothing had ever occurred to give it cause to believe that the privileges of Dr. Purcell should be suspended or restricted in any manner. On direct examination Dr. Myers, a member of the board of trustees of the hospital and a member of the hospital staff, was asked whether or not, as a member of the board, anything had come to his attention to make him believe that Dr. Purcell should have had his privileges either restricted or changed. His answer was "No." On cross-examination, Zimbelman's attorney asked the following question:

> "Q. Now, Mr. Slutes asked you, in the last question he asked, and I tried to write it down as accurately as I could, was this: 'Has anything come to your attention, as a member of the board, to make you believe that Dr. Purcell should have had his privileges either qualified or restricted or changed'? I believe the answer was no; is that correct?
>
> A. That's correct.
>
> Q. Now, Mr. Zimbelman was operated on in this case, Doctor, in April 1969. Now, before April 1969, before that date, the question of Francis Blickley came to the court; didn't it?
>
> A. Not that I recall.
>
> Q. And, Doctor, wouldn't the fact that Francis Blickley brought a lawsuit against Dr. Purcell on July 9, 1965, and that the case was actually tried in a courtroom to a judge and a jury and a judgment against Dr. Purcell was rendered on April 18, 1967 of finding a judgment that Dr. Purcell had handled the

Blickley problem in a manner below the standard of care, wouldn't that have been a fact that the board would have considered to have justified taking some action?"

[9, 10] At that point an objection was interposed. The Wolford and Kelly cases involved suits not only against Dr. Purcell but also against the hospital, yet, Dr. Myers testified that the board of trustees of Tucson General Hospital was unaware of the suits, but was willing to only say that it was very possible. The entire line of questioning as to the Blickley verdict, the amount of the Hill complaint and the Kelly and Wolford suits against both Purcell and the hospital was directly relevant to the hospital's defense of lack of knowledge of any past misdeeds on the part of Dr. Purcell. Where a hospital's alleged misconduct involves an omission to act, the hospital will not be held responsible unless it had reason to know that it should have acted within the duty it concededly had. [Citation omitted.] The evidence as to the Blickley, Hill, Kelly and Wolford suits was clearly admissible to prove that the hospital had reason to know or should have known of the conduct of Dr. Purcell.

· · ·

Affirmed.

TUCSON MEDICAL CENTER, INC. v. MISEVCH
113 Ariz. 34, 545 P.2d 958 (1976)

HAYS, Justice.

The Tucson Medical Center (hereinafter TMC) is a defendant in a superior court action brought by Misevch against Royal Rudolph, M.D. (now deceased), Associated Anesthesiologists of Tucson, and TMC. Misevch claims that Rudolph was negligent in administering anesthesia to Misevch's wife during surgery at TMC for the removal of a low back disc as a result of which she suffered cardiac arrest and brain damage and later died. The complaint alleges that Rudolph was under the influence of alcohol and falling asleep at the time of the operation and that TMC was negligent in retaining Rudolph on its medical staff.

Misevch filed a motion to compel TMC to produce for inspection 21 groups of documents which fall into three general categories: (1) complaints or incident reports concerning Rudolph at TMC prior to the surgery; (2) reports and minutes of the medical review committees concerning the surgery; and (3) medical records of other patients of Rudolph at TMC. The trial judge ordered substantial compliance with the motion. TMC brought a special action before the Court of Appeals which declined to accept jurisdiction. A petition for review was then filed in this court which granted the petition. Thereafter, pursuant to Rule 1, Rules of Procedure for Special Actions, this court accepted jurisdiction of a petition for special action, but would not allow oral argument thereon. We consolidated the special action with the petition for review and now remand the case for proceedings not inconsistent with the following opinion.

[1–3] Hospitals have been given and have accepted the duty of supervising the competence of the doctors on their staffs. *Purcell v. Zimbelman*, 18 Ariz. App. 75, 500 P.2d 335 (1972), *review denied;* . . . The concept of corporate responsibility for the quality of medical care was clearly enunciated in *Darling v. Charleston Community Memorial Hospital*, 33 Ill. 2d 326, 211 N. E. 2d 253, 14 A. L. R. 3d 860 (1965), when that court held that hospitals and their governing bodies may be held liable for injuries resulting from negligent supervision of members of their medical staffs. [Citation omitted.] The hospital has assumed certain responsibilities for the care of its patients and it must meet the standards of responsibility commensurate with this trust. [Citation omitted.] If the medical staff was negligent in the exercise of its duty of supervising its members or in failing to recommend action by the hospital's governing body prior to the case in issue, then the hospital would be negligent. [Citation omitted.]

[4] When the hospital's alleged negligence is predicated on an omission to act, the hospital will not be held respon-

sible unless it had reason to know that it should have acted within its duty to the patient to see to it that only professionally competent persons were on its staff. [Citation omitted.] Therefore, its knowledge, actual or constructive, is an essential factor in determining whether or not the hospital exercised reasonable care or was guilty of negligence. [Citation omitted.]

To guarantee the proper review of medical practices within hospitals, the legislature enacted A. R. S. § 36–445 et seq.

> "The governing body of each licensed hospital shall require that physicians admitted to practice in the hospital organize into committees to review the professional practices within the hospital for the purposes of reducing morbidity and mortality and for the improvement of the care of patients provided in the institution. Such review shall include the nature, quality and necessity of the care provided and the preventability of complications and deaths occurring in the hospital." A. R. S. § 36–445.

[5] The statutory scheme provides that certain information considered by the medical staff review committee is subject to subpoena to be delivered for the inspection of a judge who shall determine what material is relevant and competent. A. R. S. § 36–445.01. This is the statute within which the trial judge acted in this case and which is now questioned. Review has been made difficult, however, by the inadequate record in this case. In passing upon the claim raised, a reviewing court should have the documents before it which allow the court to match the medical staff committee's function with the specifications of the statute; the record in this case is completely deficient. [Citation omitted.]

[6, 7] The information considered by the committees is subject to subpoena except where a medical legal panel is formally available. If such a panel is available, the information is given only to it. The panel is defined in A. R. S. § 36–445.01(C) as comprising an equal number of attorneys and physicians to review alleged medical malpractice claims.

. . .

[8, 9] A medical-legal panel not being available, the *information considered* by the committee is, in accord with A. R. S. § 36-445.01(A):

> ". . . subject to subpoena but shall be delivered by the custodian only to the judge in a judicial proceeding, who shall review such information."

Any information disclosed to the parties in the discretion of the judge shall only be disclosed in accord with the physician-patient privilege set forth in A. R. S. § 12-2235 and A. R. S. § 36-445.03. Evidence privileged within the statute remains privileged even if transcribed into hospital records or the privilege would be meaningless. [Citation omitted.] Concomitantly, when neither the physician nor the patient has an interest in the proceedings, the hospital has standing to assert the privilege to protect the absent patient. [Citations omitted.]

. . . The Arizona statute should not, however, discourage the full and frank giving of information to a review committee . . . in the light of A. R. S. § 36-445.02 which provides that:

> "A person who without malice and in good faith . . . furnishes any records, information or assistance to [a review] committee is not subject to liability for civil damages or any legal action in consequence thereof."

Statements made immediately after an occurrence are unique and can never be duplicated precisely. [Citation omitted.] The trial judge will make the proper determination of relevancy. [Statutory citation omitted.]

[10] We make the distinction . . . that the proper demarcation is between purely factual, investigative matters and materials which are the product of reflective deliberation or policy-making processes. Statements and information considered by the committee are subject to subpoena for the determinations of the trial judge, but the reports and minutes of the medical review committees are not.

[Citation omitted.] This has been established by the Arizona Legislature as a matter of public policy in this state. The statute only permits the subpoena of "information considered by the committees"...but does not refer to the minutes and reports of those committees. The protection is justified by the overwhelming public interest in maining the confidentiality of the medical staff meetings so that the discussion can freely flow to further the care and treatment of patients. [Citation omitted.]

. . . Bearing the delegated responsibility for review, the candor of the members is necessary in the consideration of their colleagues' skills towards objectively regulating privileges, and the quality of treatment so depends. [Citation omitted.]

> "Confidentiality is essential to effective functioning of these staff meetings; and these meetings are essential to the continued improvement in the care and treatment of patients. Candid and conscientious evaluation of clinical practices is a *sine qua non* of adequate hospital care. To subject these discussions and deliberations to the discovery process, without a showing of exceptional necessity, would result in terminating such deliberations. Constructive professional criticism cannot occur in an atmosphere of apprehension that one doctor's suggestion will be used as a denunciation of a colleague's conduct in a malpractice suit." [Citation omitted.]

[11] Furthermore, the medical review of a procedure is not a part of current patient care, but is a retrospective discussion of treatment and, absent extraordinary circumstances, there is no good cause for disclosure in light of the considerable public interest to the contrary. [Citation omitted.]

The case is remanded for proceedings not inconsistent with this opinion.

CAMERON, C. J., STRUCKMEYER, V. C. J., and HOLOHAN and GORDON, JJ., concur.

PEDERSON v. DUMOUCHEL
72 Wash. 2d 73, 431 P.2d 973, 31 A.L.R.3d 1100 (1967)

[2] ... [W]e conclude that it is negligence as a matter of law for a hospital to permit a surgical operation upon a patient under general anesthetic without the presence and supervision of a medical doctor in the operating room, in the absence of extraordinary and emergent circumstances.

Our conclusion is fortified by the fact that the hospital permitted the breach of one of its own rules.

> Patients requiring dental service may be coadmitted by a member of the medical staff and a local dentist who is qualified, legally, professionally and ethically to practice here. The former shall perform an adequate medical examination prior to dental surgery, and be responsible for the patient's medical care. Rule and Regulation No. 5 of St. Joseph Hospital, p. 16.

Dr. Dumouchel did not assume the responsibility "for the patient's medical care" while in surgery.

The judgment dismissing this action against the hospital is reversed, and the case is remanded for a new trial limited to a determination of whether the hospital's negligence was a proximate cause of plaintiff's injury, if any, and if so, the amount of damages.

Comment on the Cases

Depending on how one looks at the hospital's responsibility, these cases either represent new law or are merely extensions of older law to fit current problems.

Since law is conceived to be guidelines for future behavior, what are the various interplays of the parties' rights and duties when hospitals do what these holdings direct? Is it appropriate for a hospital to remove a physician's hospital privileges to practice there, when he still holds a valid state license to practice medicine in that state? Does this place the hospital in a position superior to the state in the regulation of medical practice in the state? Should it?

When one recognizes the difference between legal causation and medical causation, does a medical malpractice suit, if won by the plaintiff, become the equivalent of incompetence? How many malpractice suits add up to incompetence? What is incompetence? What are the elements of incompetence?

Is the "Rule and Regulation No. 5" in the *Pederson* case clear on its face? Could Dr. Dumouchel realistically have assumed responsibility for the patient's anesthetic care if he were an anesthesiologist? A surgeon? An internist? Pediatrician, dermatologist, or psychiatrist? What is Rule No. 5 intended to accomplish? How is it intended to accomplish it? Is the method appropriate? How shall the hospital oversee the rule? How shall the hospital enforce the rule: (a) to respond to a catastrophe; or (b) to prevent harm? How would you write Rule No. 5 to accomplish the purpose?

The following material is excerpted from Chapter XII, Hospital Liability, in Arthur F. Southwick's *The Law of Hospital and Health Care Administration*, Health Administration Press, University of Michigan Press, Ann Arbor, 1978. Professor Southwick looks at the changing physician-hospital relationship from the point of view of a lawyer and a business administrator. You will find that he demolishes a few long cherished legal ideas.

Hospital Liability

Following the rapid decline of charitable immunity from liability for tort during the 1950s and 1960s, hospital liability has been one of the most dramatically changing areas of personal injury law. ... The focus here is on the nonprofit hospital and the duties owed the patient or visitor in jurisdictions which have removed all charitable immunities. Most states have now adopted full liability with respect to the voluntary hospital.

The Nature and Role of the Community Hospital

Even after the abolishment of charitable immunity, many courts regarded a community hospital as a mere facility, or hotel, whose reason for existence was simply to provide a place where a licensed physician practiced medicine in his individual way of caring for his private patients.

In other words, the hospital was no more than a "doctor's workshop" in the minds of many lawyers and judges as well as in the view of many physicians and hospital administrators. A relatively sharp distinction was drawn between hospital services and medical services. The corporate practice of medicine rule was frequently asserted as a valid reason for this distinction. The legal duties of the hospital to the patient were accordingly quite limited, since the respective roles of the hospital and the physician or medical professional were thought to be distinctly separable.

In the 1970s there is still considerable confusion in the minds of some lawyers and medical professionals concerning the respective roles of the doctor and the hospital in caring for hospitalized patients. Nevertheless it is abundantly evident that the role and nature of the modern community hospital have been changing and will continue to change rapidly. Forward-looking physicians and professionally trained hospital administrators have openly and energetically attacked the doctor's workshop concept of the hospital. In all respects medical practice has become increasingly institutionalized, the physician depending upon the hospital and the hospital depending on the physician. It is not an overstatement to say that the practice of scientific medicine is impossible today unless the physician has access to a hospital. The practice of medicine is increasingly hospital-oriented; specialization of practice and the individual physician's increasing need for consultation with specialists lead inevitably to institutionalization. Meanwhile the medical profession has also developed techniques of auditing hospital care, whereby peer groups of physicians evaluate the medical performance of colleagues in the interest of raising the standards of patient care.

The services provided the community by the hospital and its medical staff have continually expanded. Instead of confining its role to the care of acutely ill patients, the modern community hospital now renders a wide range of services formerly provided by others or not provided at all. The public has become increasingly sophisticated in demanding excellent care and an increased range of services. The great growth in insurance coverage and third-party financing arrangements since World War II has contributed significantly to this aspect of the changing role of the hospital. The hospital's out-patient services and its role in the diagnosis of illness — as contrasted with acute care — are far more important today than a decade or two ago. Hospital emergency rooms render more and more services; indeed, the emergency room is often utilized by the public in place of a doctor's office. Hospitals are now developing home care and preventive health programs and are entering into contractual arrangements with nursing homes and other institutions for long-term care.

The institutionalization of medical practice and the increasing range of hospital services to the community have meant that salary arrangements between the hospital and professional persons have been increasing in number and importance. For example, it is not now unusual to find a chief of the medical staff, or a medical director, being paid a full- or part-time salary to compensate him for his institutional responsibilities. Formerly a licensed physician had few institutional responsibilities, but modern medical practice and the development of the hospital as a community health center have greatly increased the ties between the corporate hospital and the doctor.

Adequate medical administration has actually been lacking in many community hospitals despite the fact that the care of patients is the central function of a hospital. Medical administration cannot be accomplished by busy private practitioners devoting to administration only the little time that remains after attending their patients. A designated physician is clearly needed who will assume authority delegated by the hospital governing body for medical administration and who will report to and be accountable to the board of trustees through the hospital's chief executive officer.

This person, whether his title is chief of staff or medical director, has both overall authority for hospital-medical staff relationships and operational direction of all clinical departments. Specifically he coordinates the planning and development of health care programs for the hospital, provides administrative direction for heads of the clinical departments as well as staff support to the governing board and the organized medical staff, maintains professional liaison with the nursing staff and other professionals who support the practice of medicine, and participates actively in improving the hospital's relations with other organizations and professional associations. Thus professionals now recognize that a hospital does not consist of two organizations — one a business entity and the other a medical center. Rather, *hospitals are single organizations whose purpose is to arrange for and to a large extent control the delivery of total patient care in accordance with recognized professional standards* [italics added].

Licensure of medical and paramedical personnel is not a satisfactory legal vehicle for controlling the quality of medical care. In the first place licensure statutes specify only minimal qualifications for practice and cannot measure competence for medical and surgical specialization. Secondly, the statutes provide no satisfactory method of assuring the continuing competence of an individual over the years; periodic review of competence and educational qualifications is seldom conducted under the licensure statutes, and relicensure is not required. The enforcement and disciplinary powers of the governmental administrative agencies responsible for licensure are limited. Revocation or suspension of a license to practice are relatively rare events.

Since for these reasons licensure of professional individuals cannot be depended on to improve the quality of medical care and allied care, the American voluntary hospital system and the medical profession, to their great credit, have together assumed the burdens of raising standards and promoting excellence in the care of patients.

In their efforts to raise standards and to bring the best of American medicine to the public, the hospitals have been immeasurably aided by several national voluntary organizations which have promulgated and enforced standards. At the forefront has been the Joint Commission of Accreditation of Hospitals, whose member organizations are the American Medical Association, the American Hospital Association, the American College of Surgeons, and the American College of Physicians. In other words, the shortcomings of the licensure laws have been admirably made up for by the hospitals and voluntary professional organizations.

Neither this central role of the hospitals in establishing, maintaining, and improving standards of medical care nor the rapidly changing role of the community hospital have been overlooked by the courts. The law of hospital liability has expanded and developed because the role of the hospital in the community has changed in the past two decades and will continue to evolve. If a hospital is a single corporate organization responsible to the community for the delivery of total health care, the medical staff of the hospital is ethically and legally answerable to the corporate board of trustees in that the board becomes ultimately responsible for medical staff appointments and privileges, the rights and responsibilities provided for in the medical staff bylaws, and the discipline of staff. In other words, professionals in medicine and hospital administration, courts, and legislatures have now recognized that the corporate institution is ultimately responsible for standards of hospital medical care. This ultimate responsibility cannot be delegated by the governing body of the corporation to the medical staff. Accordingly, if the hospital fails to exercise adequate control over medical staff appointments and privileges, fails to "supervise" the attending physician in certain circumstances where the patient is in jeopardy, fails to require the attending doctor to seek consultation with specialists, or even fails to remove the doctor from a case in extreme situations, the result may be hospital liability. Such liability is avoided in the modern hospital by an organized system of peer group evaluation of medical staff performance.

The establishment and the maintenance of professional standards in the hospital consequently become a joint effort of lay hospital administration and medical staff. Lay administrators cannot ignore medical standards without great legal peril, as will be demonstrated. No longer can the business administration of a hospital be neatly separated from medical administration. The authority, as distinct from responsibility for direct and immediate control of medical standards, has to be delegated of course to the medical staff by the board of trustees. But the medical staff must then be held accountable for its delegated authority. In liability cases no real purpose is served—and certainly the quality of care is not improved—when the hospital blames the doctor, or the doctor blames the hospital and its employed personnel. As medical care becomes more institutionalized and the role of the hospital in controlling quality more central, the hospital's defenses grounded on the traditional legal doctrines of independent contractor and borrowed servant are more frequently circumvented by the courts in liability cases. The long-standing dichotomy between a community hospital's medical staff and its lay administration must be eliminated both in the interests of patients' care and to reduce the exposure of the institution to liability.

Sincere, diligent efforts are being made by hospital administrators and institutionally oriented physicians to minimize the traditional separation between hospital administration on the one hand and clinical medicine on the other.[1] The concept that the hospital as a corporate institution must establish, maintain, and be ultimately responsible for the standards of medical care practiced within its walls is recognized by the Joint Commission on Accreditation of Hospitals and by some public licensing authorities responsible for the licensure of hospitals. The jury may consider such standards to be evidence of expected performance by hospital personnel and medical staff.[2] This extension of corporate or institutional responsibility to the patient has also been forcefully recognized in several more recent judicial cases, by rules and regulations of federal programs for financing medical care, and by the statutory law of several jurisdictions. . . .

· · ·

[Footnotes renumbered.]
[1]See, for example, C. W. Eisele, M.D. (ed.), *The Medical Staff in the Modern Hospital* (New York: McGraw Hill Co., 1967).
[2]*Darling v. Charleston Community Hospital*, 33 Ill. 2d 326, 211 N.E.2d 253 (1965), *cert. denied*, 383 U.S. 946, *aff'g*, 50 Ill. App. 2d 253, 200 N.E.2d 149 (1964).

Liability for Injuries to Patients:
Two Theories

Hospital liability is fundamentally based on either corporate (institutional) negligence or vicarious liability. The latter, of course, is the doctrine of respondeat superior, which literally translated means "let the master answer." Both theories of liability have been expanded by judicial decision during recent years and each will be discussed separately.

Historically these two theories of hospital liability are separate and distinct from each other. Corporate or institutional negligence is the breach of a duty owed directly to the patient by the hospital. On the other hand, liability founded upon respondeat superior is imposed upon the hospital when an agent or servant (an employee) has been negligent within the scope of his or her employment and thereby caused injury to a third person. The employer has not been negligent or at fault; accordingly it is sometimes said that vicarious liability is "nonfault" liability, an accurate statement in the sense that the employer has not directly or personally violated any duty owed to the third person.

. . . [C]ourts and commentators have sometimes so confused or misapplied these two separate doctrines that they have become nearly merged or even indistinguishable in relation to a given set of facts involving multiple corporate or individual professional defendants. At least one can say that liability to the patient on the part of the hospital is likely, regardless of the theory argued by the plaintiff, as long as the trial establishes that either institutional standards or professional standards articulated by medical or other professional practitioners were breached and that the breach of standards was the proximate cause of injury to the patient. . . .

One should always remember that even if an employer is found to be liable under the doctrine of respondeat superior the employee who committed the tort can also be held individually and personally liable for the injuries caused by his or her wrongful act or omission. Hospital employees are more and more often joined as defendants in liability suits along with their employer. When vicarious liability applies, the liability of the employer and employee is joint and several. This means that the aggrieved plaintiff may sue any one or more of the parties separately or all of them together at his option, obtain a court judgment against all the defendants, and collect the judgment in whole from one or in part from each of the defendants. The plaintiff is not, of course, permitted to collect each judgment in full from two or more defendants; in other words he may not collect double (or more) damages to compensate for his injuries. If the plaintiff collects the judgment in whole or in part from the employer, in theory the employer in turn has the right of indemnification from the negligent employee. Sometimes this right is asserted when the employer and employee are insured against liability by different insurance carriers.

. . .

Three Traditional Corporate or Institutional Duties

In corporate negligence, although human error or omission is involved, it is the hospital itself as an entity or a corporate institution that is negligent, and liability attaches directly to the hospital. The hospital owes a defined legal duty directly to the patient or visitor, and the duty is not delegable to the medical staff or other personnel. A Connecticut court once defined the corporate negligence of a hospital in these words: "Corporate negligence is the failure of those entrusted with the task of providing accommodations and facilities necessary to carry out the charitable purpose of the corporation to follow in a given situation the established standard of conduct to which the corporation should conform."[3]

Accordingly, the legal question is this: what duties does the hospital owe directly to the patient or visitor? To answer this query, we must consider the corporate pur-

---

[3]*Bader v. United Orthodox Synagogue*, 148 Conn. 449, 453, 172 A.2d 192, 194 (1961).

poses of a community hospital. Does a hospital — or should a hospital — restrict its function and role to furnishing physical facilities and accommodations wherein private physicians care for and treat their patients? In other words, is a hospital nothing more than a "doctor's workshop"? If so, the duties owed directly to the patient by the hospital can justifiably be quite narrow and limited. Historically this has been the general attitude of the courts in corporate negligence cases.

On the other hand, if a hospital has broader purposes its corporate duties can be expected to be broader. As we noted at the outset of this discussion, the nature and role of the hospital vis-a-vis the community has indeed been broadening in recent years. Hospitals are doing more than providing physical facilities for the practice of medicine. In response to public demand, and encouraged by leaders in the medical-health care professions, hospitals are gradually becoming true community health centers. The developments will continue and accelerate in the decades ahead. In time, hospitals will become the focus for providing the community with the entire range of medical care — preventive as well as curative, out-patient care as well as care for acute illnesses demanding hospitalization. Hospitals are, and for the foreseeable future will continue to be, the primary vehicle for controlling and raising standards of quality of care. Hence court decisions in liability cases are likely to recognize the changing and central role of the hospital and gradually expand judicial concepts of corporate negligence.

· · ·

Negligence in Selecting and Retaining Medical Staff

The tendency to institutionalize liability, noted earlier in connection with the doctrine of respondeat superior, is even more apparent under the second of the two theories of hospital liability mentioned early in this chapter, namely, the violation of a duty owed directly by the institution to the patient. Application of this theory has constituted a direct attack upon the existing dichotomy between hospital management and medical staff. Prior to the landmark case of *Darling v. Charleston Community Memorial Hospital*, decided by the Supreme Court of Illinois in 1965,[4] the case law recognized only very limited direct duties owed by the hospital to the patient. The *Darling* decision was destined to change that. It gave impetus to a legal clarification of the respective roles of hospital trustees, administration, and medical staff.

A young man named Darling suffered a fractured leg while playing football and was brought to the Charleston Community Memorial Hospital's emergency room where he was attended by Dr. Alexander, the staff physician on call. He was thereafter admitted to the hospital as a patient of Dr. Alexander's. Then the grim series of events leading to the lawsuit occurred: the doctor's dilemmas regarding a constricted cast which was causing circulatory difficulties; the patient's continual pain and complaints; the nurses' knowledge of clinical difficulties and their failure to communicate them to hospital administration; Dr. Alexander's failure to call for a consultation, as arguably required by a medical staff bylaw; the failure of the chief of staff or the hospital administrator to seek enforcement of the bylaw; and, finally, the removal of the patient to Barnes Hospital in St. Louis, by which time it was too late to save the injured leg.

Suit was brought against both the physician and the hospital. The former settled the claim against him and was dismissed as a defendant in the litigation. The case against the hospital was taken to trial, and a jury found in favor of the plaintiff. Allegations against the institution included claims that it had permitted an unqualified physician to do orthopedic surgery, that the hospital failed to require periodic reports from a medical staff tissue committee in order to determine qualifications and privileges of individual physicians practicing within the hospital, and that the hospital administration knew from the nurses' daily reports that the patient's case was difficult, yet made no

---

[4] 33 Ill. 2d 326, 211 N.E.2d 253, 14 A.L.R.3d 860 (1965), *cert. denied*, 383 U.S. 946 (1966).

attempt to correct the situation. The administration acknowledged that the hospital had done little or nothing to review the doctor's qualifications for orthopedic practice since he obtained his license to practice medicine in 1928; further, it appeared that Dr. Alexander had not been responsible for the care of a major leg fracture for several years.

In support of the allegations, the plaintiff was permitted to introduce into evidence the Standards of the Joint Commission on the Accreditation of Hospitals to the effect that the hospital board of trustees is ultimately responsible for the standards of patient care; the Illinois Department of Public Health regulations under the Hospital Licensing Act to the same effect; and the medical staff bylaws of Charleston Community Hospital, which required attending physicians to seek consultation with specialists in "problem cases." The hospital defended on the general basis that it was prohibited from practicing medicine under the law, that it was therefore powerless to forbid or command any act of a licensed physician. The hospital further relied on the prevailing standards, custom, and practice of hospitals in the local community as a defense of its position.

The Illinois Supreme Court ultimately upheld the jury verdict against the hospital as supportable either because (1) the hospital failed to have a sufficient number of trained nurses capable of recognizing and bringing the patient's worsening condition to the attention of hospital administration and medical staff, so that consultation could be secured, or because (2) the hospital failed to review the treatment rendered to plaintiff and to require consultation as needed.[5] Thus, the doctrine of respondeat superior was at most an alternate basis for the court's holding;[6] the

---

[5]Id. at 333, 211 N.E.2d at 258.
[6]See *Goff v. Doctor's General Hospital of San Jose*, 166 Cal. App. 2d 314, 333 P.2d 29 (Dist. Ct. App. 1958). (A hospital was liable when nurses who knew a patient was suffering serious bleeding tried without success to reach her private physician and then failed to report to administration so that another physician could be called.) Accord with *Darling* that nurses have a duty to monitor a patient's condition with reasonable care, to recognize a

hospital's independent negligence – alone – would be sufficient to impose liability.

The decision raises directly the issue of the respective roles of the hospital administration, the nursing staff, and the medical staff. The jury verdict against the hospital was permitted to stand even though plaintiff presented no precise, expert testimony that failure to review the qualifications of medical staff members or failure to require consultation actually caused plaintiff's injury. Thus some observers have contended that the case was unfortunate because it gave the jury an unwarranted opportunity to sympathize with the plaintiff and in the process to distort and further confuse the role of the hospital administration. Without doubt the facts and evidence at trial aroused considerable sympathy for young Darling's plight; in the language of lawyers the facts showed a "hard case."

However, the *Darling* decision should not be interpreted as meaning that lay individuals in hospital administration are now called upon to control the clinical practice of medicine on a case-by-case basis. Clearly the court does not require this; such lay control would be intolerable because only physicians can exercise clinical judgment. Rather, the court simply considered the "hospital" to be one organization – the administration and medical staff sharing jointly the responsiblity for standards of care. The administration, represented by the board of trustees and the lay administrator, is now called upon to stimulate the medical staff of the institution to organize a means of re-

---

deteriorating condition, to report to the attending physician, and if he is unavailable or unresponsive to report to the hospital administration so that appropriate action may be taken: *Collins v. Westlake Community Hospital,* 57 Ill. 2d 388, 312 N.E.2d 614 (1974), and *Karrigan v. Nazareth Convent and Academy,* 212 Kan. 44, 510 P.2d 190 (1973). See also: *Garfield Park Community Hospital v. Vitacco,* 327 N.E.2d 408 (Ill. App. 1975). (The hospital settled a claim alleging that nurses were negligent in failing to observe and report symptoms of impaired circulation. Even if the patient's attending physician was concurrently personally negligent, the hospital was not entitled to indemnity from the physician, since the nurses were employees and the physician not an employee of the hospital.)

viewing the professional qualifications and performance of each individual staff physician. The physicians appointed to the hospital staff must have an established procedure for consultation, and lines of communication between clinical practice and lay administration must be open. The medical staff is held accountable to the corporate organization for standards of medical care. The chief of the medical staff must be a dedicated individual, essentially institutionally oriented, and devoted to implementing standards promulgated by responsible private and public agencies which accredit and license hospitals in the public interest. In other words, fragmentation and individualism within the walls of the hospital must be reduced insofar as is humanly possible. In this light, the case can be approved simply because it focuses on the obligation of the hospital through an organized medical staff to exercise control of standards of practice.

The case further indicates that legal doctrine should finally and forcefully reject the antiquated, rather meaningless notion that a corporation cannot practice medicine. To be sure, only a physician can exercise clinical judgment, but the realities of modern medical care clearly indicate that the doctor can practice adequately only with institutional affiliation and support. It can be asserted that the "corporate practice of medicine" rule as enunciated in the past in some cases and statutes has no relevance today to a nonprofit hospital striving for high standards of professional excellence.

The result of the *Darling* case is consistent with the views and attitudes of professionals concerned with the role of the modern hospital. It is consistent with the realities of modern clinical practice and the institutionalization of medical care. The welfare of hospitalized patients requires collective concern. The hospital is properly highlighted as the focal point for providing and coordinating medical care for the community and as the best available vehicle for controlling and improving standards of care. Hence, the real impact of the case is that it calls attention to the need for an organized medical staff willing and capable of accounting to itself and to the hospital for standards of care.

• • •

Summary — Institutional Liability One Way or the Other

What the recent liability cases add up to in a final analysis is this: the historical distinction between the two presumably separate legal theories underlying hospital liability has been all but obliterated. Appellate courts are to an increasing extent failing to discriminate clearly between corporate or institutional negligence and respondeat superior or vicarious liability. This is not for want of clear thinking or of scholarship, but simply the result of factual realities. The first of these realities is the increase in all sorts of malpractice and personal injury suits in a claims-conscious society. More significant to this discussion is the reality in the hospital-medical world that health care is increasingly delivered to the public through hospitals and similar institutions. There is an irresistible tendency to hold the institution responsible when things go wrong and when negligence can be established as the proximate cause of injury.

Accordingly, in litigation presenting genuine issues of an employment relationship, the doctrine of respondeat superior, the following legal developments have occurred. First, the doctrine has been applied to situations involving professional employees and their negligent acts, rather than being confined to "administrative" acts. Second, the notion of apparent or ostensible agency was developed to allow a plaintiff to recover damages against a hospital which "held out" or made it appear that the negligent actor was an employee, when in fact he was not. Third, the borrowed-servant doctrine is disappearing, thereby placing vicarious liability on the hospital and not on the physician alone for the negligent act of an intern, resident, or nurse. And finally, . . . there is a forthright finding of an employment relationship between hospital and doctor, even though the parties involved certainly considered their relationship to be otherwise. . . . The independent contractor defense can no longer be successfully raised by the hospital, except in limited circumstances where it is explicitly established that the negligent act which caused injury was performed solely by the doctor, and where a patient has expressly and voluntarily employed the physician privately.

In cases presenting issues of a hospital's negligence in failing to monitor the quality of care rendered by members of its medical staff ... the trend is clear. The organized medical staff and its committees act on behalf of the hospital. Their negligent omissions become the hospital's omissions. Institutional liability can thus be established in the hospital as long as adequate proof of proximate cause can be established.

Additional Reading

Blumstein, J. F., Constitutional Perspectives on Governmental Discussions Affecting Human Life and Health. *Law and Contemporary Problems* 40 (1976):231–305.

Carlson, R. J., Health Manpower Licensing and Emerging Institutional Responsibility for the Quality of Care. *Law and Contemporary Problems* 35 (1970): 849–878.

Forgotson, E. H. and Cook, J. L., Innovations and Experiments in Uses of Health Manpower—the Effect of Licensure Laws. *Law and Contemporary Problems* 32 (1967):731–750.

Mechanic, D. The Changing Structure of Medical Practice. *Law and Contemporary Problems* 32 (1967):707–730.

Mechanic, D. *Public Expectations and Health Care.* New York: John Wiley & Sons, Inc., 1972.

Priest, A. J. G., Possible Adaptation of Public Utility Concepts in the Health Care Field, *Law and Contemporary Problems* 35 (1970): 839–848.

Chapter Nine

Administrative Law and the Administrative Process

IX

Administrative law began developing some eighty to ninety years ago and therefore it is not so well honed as the law of torts or the law of contracts, but it is better honed than the law of informed consent. The history of the intriguing social and political struggles leading to an administrative agency's creation is gripping to read, but administrative law in and of itself tends to be dry and dusty. Nevertheless, this body of law is becoming increasingly important to the physician because society at this time has chosen to command the direction and content of medical care. Administrative agencies are being used to direct and implement that social policy.

To the physician, administrative law is likely to be either an amorphous concept or an unknown. But, because of the federal government's increasing purchases of medical care, the physician can expect to be caught up more and more in the intricacies of the administrative process. So widespread and pervasive is the use of the administrative process in our government that one legal commentator is led to say, "...contemporary social scientists, with increasing regularity, describe America as an administrative state. The distinguishing quality of the modern administrative state is its reliance upon the administrative process as a principal instrumentality for the achievement of national policies."[1]

This chapter is intended to orient the physician to administrative law and the administrative process so that he will be able to understand the currently developing field of medical administrative law (as exemplified by Medicare and Medicaid). Lest the following material seem too abstruse or abstract, the preceding chapter, The Hospital and The Physician, can be looked at as a microcosm of the administrative

---

[1]J. O. Freedman *Crisis and Legitimacy: The Administrative Process and American Government*. London and New York: Cambridge University Press, 1978, p. 3.

process. By-laws set forth policy statements, organizational matters, and rules and regulations. Setting up clinical departments in a hospital is an example of organizational matters; granting hospital privileges is a licensing procedure; disciplinary hearings are adjudications; and, finally, there are provisions for internal and judiciary appeals.

Administrative Law

In his Administrative Law Treatise, Davis defines administrative law, "...as the law that governs the powers and procedures of the agencies. Administrative law is about the machinery of government. It includes procedural law created by the agencies but not the substantive law created by them, such as tax law, labor law...."[2] He defines an agency as "...a governmental body, other than a court and other than a legislative body, which affects the rights of private parties through either adjudication or rule making."[3]

The important words in the latter definition are "affects the rights of private parties." This concept is of paramount importance because when a private party's rights are affected, the governmental body affecting those rights must afford the private party both substantive and procedural due process.

The Administrative Process

Under well established legal principles, those who have rights and powers can delegate them, but they cannot delegate their accompanying responsibilities. Hence, if the congress or other legislature has the responsibility and the accompanying power to regulate the subject matter under scrutiny, then the legislature can delegate its power and rights to regulate the subject matter to an administrative agency or commission, but it remains both constitutionally and politically accountable to its electorate for the subject matter delegated. Note

---

[2]K. C. Davis *Administrative Law Treatise.* San Diego: University of San Diego, 2nd Ed., Vol. 1, p. 2.
[3]Ibid, p. 9.

that the commissioners or board members of an agency do not have to stand for election every two or six years as do the representatives and senators who created the agency. Nevertheless, time has shown that public interest in and public surveillance of an agency's activities, or the subject matter under its jurisdiction, assures optimum performance of the agency. When such interest wanes, the performance of the agency may or may not deteriorate.

It has been pointed out, somewhat cynically, that ". . . administrative agencies are created to deal with current crises, or with emerging problems, requiring supervision and flexibility,"[4] or those problems ". . . not amenable to legislative stricture."[5] In other words, in addition to the needs for continuing supervision and flexibility to adjust to changing conditions (such as interstate commerce), (i) the subject matter considered to require governmental regulation is of a narrow and highly specialized nature (such as radio and television channels); (ii) such situations requiring regulation demand an intimate knowledge of both the industry or subject matter under the agency's jurisdiction and its dynamics in the marketplace; and, finally, (iii) when a legislature decides it not only has insufficient time now to gain the expertise needed to address the problem adequately, but also will have insufficient time in the future to continuously supervise the industry or subject matter, the legislature then forms an agency or commission to handle the problem.

Operational independence lets the agency tailor its organization and procedures in order to carry out its legislative mandate to regulate the industry or subject matter delegated to it.

Once the legislature recognizes the need for an agency, it is created (i) by statute, (ii) by executive order authorized by statute, or (iii) by state constitutional provision. Note that, although the federal government uses administrative agencies extensively, the United States Constitution does not mention administrative agencies. As a result, the legitimacy of the federal administrative process has been sharply challenged in the past. However, the United States Supreme Court has upheld the federal government's use of the administrative process as an appropriate legislative tool.

In general, members of an administrative agency have expertise in

---

[4]E. Gellhorn *Administrative Law in a Nutshell*. St. Paul, Minn.: West Publishing Co., 1972, p. 1.
[5]Ibid, p. 3.

the subject matter or industry under the agency's jurisdiction, and, usually, the same political philosophy as the person or persons who nominate and confirm them. This is merely a fact of political life. In many cases, the only source of sufficient numbers of persons who have the requisite expertise to allow the agency to fulfill its legislative mandate is the industry under regulation. Under these conditions, either an intentional or unconscious coziness can develop between the regulators and the regulated. This makes it difficult to find enough superior administrators who can make the hard decisions against the regulated, follow the legislative mandate, and act in the best interests of the public. Freedman explains that ". . . expertise and independence were seen as compensatory substitutes for political accountability."[6] Furthermore, "[b]y granting administrative agencies an effective independence from the normal political processes, Congress would ensure that administrators were free to be impartial in their judgments, guided by their most conscientious visions of what constituted wise regulation, and committed only to protecting the public interest."[7]

Rulemaking

For the ease of initial analysis, the work of an agency can be split into two parts, rulemaking and adjudication. Rulemaking looks forward and is in essence legislation by the agency to fulfill its legislative mandate (for example, the Interstate Commerce Commission's rules and regulations that set railroad freight tariffs); adjudication looks backward and is essentially a trial and, if indicated, punishment.

A legislature's delegation of power and authority to an agency lets it organize itself, set out its rules of procedure, issue policy statements as to how the agency plans to effectuate its legislative mandate, and issue rules and regulations that not only regulate the subject matter under its jurisdiction but also have the force of law. Articulation of rules and regulations within its delegated jurisdiction that have the force of law is legislation. Note that these rules and regulations are not arrived at

---

[6]J. O. Freedman *Crisis and Legitimacy: The Administrative Process and American Government.* London and New York: Cambridge University Press, 1978, p. 76.
[7]Ibid, p. 60.

by a majority vote of politically accountable legislators, but by independent agency personnel according to procedures that they themselves set up and are using.

Rulemaking can be carried out (1) by an agency acting on its own (by agency fiat); (2) on notice given and comments (oral or written) called for; and (3) in a formal trial-type hearing. The Federal Administrative Procedure Act (APA) or similar state statutes and judicial decisions determine what methods are permissible for procedural matters, interpretive statements, or regulations. As a rough rule of thumb, if an agency's contemplated rulemaking will affect a private party's rights, that private party has the right to be heard by the agency concerning that impending rulemaking, regardless of label applied.

Adjudication

The following step in the administrative process is referred to as adjudication. Should a regulated transgress a rule or regulation, the agency or commission can investigate, hold a hearing, make a determination of guilt or innocence, and mete out the appropriate punishment. Again, note that the agency acts both as accuser and as judge, which runs counter to the traditional Anglo-American concept of separating the accuser and the judge.

The formality of agency adjudication procedures runs the gamut from what amounts to a formal trial, with all the rules of evidence and procedure, to the so-called "informal action," which is in essence summary punishment. The latter procedure may be no more than an informal meeting between agency personnel and a representative of the regulated company that has transgressed a regulation. These two hammer out a solution *without* formal rules either of law or of the agency being observed, and no record or transcript of the meeting is kept. Such lack of records renders appeal most difficult.

If the regulated is unsuccessful in his defense of the alleged transgression, he must first exhaust his intra-agency route of appeal before pursuing an appeal in the courts.

The Road Ahead

Physicians on hospital medical care evaluation committees, as well as the hospital staff physicians, should look at each regulation or rule or letter of transmittal under discussion from two separate and distinct aspects. The obvious aspect is the contents of the rule, or regulation, or letter of transmittal. The physician may overlook or only hazily perceive the other aspect, administrative law, which is really an exercise in statutory interpretation. What is the rule, regulation, or letter of transmittal intended to accomplish? Is its aim proper or appropriate? Is its method of accomplishing that aim appropriate? Finally, does that rule affect the rights of third parties; and, if it does, have those third parties been heard by the agency before that rule, regulation, or letter of transmittal was promulgated?

Other procedural questions arise. By what warrant do third-party payors determine what surgical operations they will and will not pay for? Some subsidiary questions are: just how much sub-delegation of agency powers is permitted? Do those to whom the agency delegates its powers have to follow and obey the same procedural rules of the APA and of the agency itself? Are letters of transmittal ukases to circumvent the APA and the agency's own rules of procedure?

It is questions like these, in addition to the traditional tort and contract problems of medical practice, that physicians will have to wrestle with, as the federal government buys more medical care for its citizens.

Table of Cases

(Listings are alphabetical)

Index

About the Author

Charles W. Quimby, Jr., is an Associate Professor in the Department of Anesthesiology, Vanderbilt University School of Medicine, Nashville, Tennessee. He has been affiliated with the Law School and Medical Center at the University of Arkansas. Dr. Quimby is the author of the textbook *Anesthesiology: A Manual of Concept and Management* and a contributor to the recently published *Legal Aspects of Diagnostic Imaging.* He holds an M.D. and LL.B. from the University of Pennsylvania.

A Note on the Type

The book was composed in a face called Palatino, which is a variation of Roman Transitional, designed in the middle of the eighteenth century. The book is printed on 60 pound Warren's Old Style Wove which has a shelf life of 300 years.

Composed by H & Z Typesetters, Ann Arbor, Michigan. Printed and bound by Edwards Bros.

Typography design by Janet Novick.